Don't Fear the Reaper

William Ayles, D.D.

DEDICATION

This book is dedicated to my high-school and college buddies.

William Ayles, D.D.

CONTENTS

Author's Note 5
Prologue: The Question 13
ACT ONE 25
1   All You Need is Love 27
2   Break On Through (To the Other Side) 43
3   Turn! Turn! Turn! 51
4   The Sound of Silence 57
5   Carry On Wayward Son 69
6   Stairway to Heaven 77
ACT TWO 87
7   Jesus is Just Alright 89
8   All the Way 95
9   Saved 103
10 Personal Jesus 113
11 Spirit in the Sky 121
12 (Don't Fear) The Reaper 125
THE ENCORE 131
13 The Wall 133
14 Freedom 137
15 The Power of Prayer 145
16 Sweet Sounds of Heaven 151
17 Get Together 159
18 It's the End of the World as We Know It (And I Feel Fine) 165
19 Backstage 169

Epilogue: Divine Intervention	179
Psalm 40	201
THE End: Paradise	205
THE PHOTOGRAPHS	211
Acknowledgments	212

Author's Note

Going back in time...

to dorm life (1977-1980) at The University of Connecticut (UConn), where we had a way of life: playing the stereo exceptionally loud. While playing beer (ping) pong, we would *crank* Led Zeppelin's "Stairway to Heaven," or Blue Öyster Cult's "Don't Fear the Reaper," and so on.

But, back then, I never really paid attention to the meaning and message intended by the lyricists. Now, I am. And I realize this: It is ancient wisdom in modern form.

Some songwriters explore the meaning of this life, and some explore the universal questions:
What's on the other side?
Is there life after this life?
And these questions lead straight into the heart of this book...

What if the scam is... death is final?

William Ayles, D.D.

What if the truth is... death isn't final?

The Grim Reaper is known to history as a mythological character—a skeleton cloaked in black— who symbolizes Death itself. The Reaper, armed with a scythe and an hourglass, walks the planet, waiting to come calling, to harvest life from the Earth—and collect another soul.

Don't Fear the Reaper is about melting the (real) fear of death.

Don't Fear the Reaper looks at our lives through the lens of musicians/lyricists. These lyricists are spiritual poets; they create musical art. And in the process, they open doors of perception. They reveal their own reality: spirituality found (or not...). Love and creativity guide them. And, in some cases, they attain a new place in life: "spiritual life" through timeless truth. They arrived.

As you view the lives and lyrics of the famous and infamous, consider a common thread: to find life's meaning, to look beyond this material existence, to reach into the spiritual realm, to shed light—and enable us to look at the moment, and beyond the moment, and open a window to our own souls.

This common thread—created by musicians—forms a unique voice. And their voice played into why I decided to write *Don't Fear the Reaper*.

This book arose from one conversation. A friend of mine opened her heart about her search for true spirituality—and here is the punch line: Her search excluded my search (what I believe). Conversation over. Now what?

Thinking about our conversation... I saw a common thread that extends all the way back to high school. Several of my high-school and college buddies, as well as my contemporaries echo a shared theme: *My friends exhibit spiritual curiosity, but without the traditional approaches we grew up with as kids (like going to church).*

They abhor the thought of opening a door to an institution: "church." They are turned off by the language of religious dogma.

But I also know music is a universal language. Then... I reflected on what I've known for decades: Music often expresses raw truth and true spirituality in a fundamental and profound manner. Music speaks volumes.

Let me say this...

Timeless truth is one thing...

Religious dogma is another.

The dust of history—formed by dogma—shrouds divine light and timeless truth. It's easy to find dogma; it's easy to be turned off by dogma; it's easy to mistake dogma for spirituality; it's easy to see a modern-day tragedy: to be deceived by dogma (institutional rules). In fact, Jesus Christ Himself revealed the same tragedy of His day: dogma replacing truth (as presented later in this book).

My friends reject religious dogma—yet have a spiritual curiosity.

> *Spiritual curiosity: the intellectual capacity to accept that not everything can be known by our five senses.*

Spiritual curiosity fueled this book. And this book is filled with bands and lyricists who give us refreshing honesty on spirituality. I draw upon these lyricists: their interviews and their songs. And several of these songs I played late into the night at UConn.

Back at UConn...

Something deeper was going on in my soul: I wanted to find *the* answer—not just any answer to spirituality. If there was absolute truth, I wanted to find it.

However, it was like trying to find a candle... deep within a twisting cave. As I wandered in that cave, time ticked away—and then I turned a corner. There it was: The candle (of divine light) illuminated the door of timeless truth.

I opened the door—and divine intervention followed: A new dimension of spiritual life filled my being—as if the fountain of youth itself had sprung up within my soul.

> *I had known about religious dogma, but I discovered spirituality through divine truth... through Jesus of Nazareth. And to this day, I have never looked back.*

William Ayles, D.D.

Little did I know, but after I opened the door of divine truth, my spiritual odyssey would lead me to experience divine intervention twice: first in 1980, and then again in 2000. Twice, I experienced how supernatural signs verify divine truth. (I relate some of these divine experiences in the Epilogue.)

The divine intervention of 2000 inspired me to write about pure spirituality revealed by the apostles. And now, I look to music: It is about seeing spirituality through the eyes of lyricists.

My interest in lyricists first started a long time ago—with Bob Dylan. In 1980, I discovered that he embraced Christ as his Lord. That spoke to me.

In the 1960s, the critics referred to Bob Dylan as the "voice of a generation." In the 1970s, Dylan opened the door of his heart to Christ. The "voice of a generation" had become a voice for Christ. I bought Dylan's album, *Saved*. The title song, "Saved," blew me away. He sang truth.

And in this book, I expound upon lyrical truth: The words of Jesus of Nazareth are woven among the chapters. He opened a portal of knowledge that leads to the spiritual dimension. He conveyed spiritual truth. He conveyed life's meaning. He pulled back the curtain between our life and everlasting life. The words of Jesus Christ and the songwriters

are relatable. Personally, I can relate to all of them.

To enhance the message of the songwriters, the songs have corresponding YouTube QR codes. Thereby, the lyrics come to life—turning this journey into a concert.

That said...

The Prologue introduces the book by throwing paint on the canvas about the universal question: Is there life after death? Then, 4 musicians speak about spirituality. Three songs introduce the show.

Act One presents 15 songs, which portray life's joy and mystery, and the spiritual journey: the two paths, belief... or not.

Act Two presents 9 songs—which illustrate the arrival:

> Love.
> Hope.
> Peace.
> Truth.
> Knowing.
> Spirituality.
> Deliverance.
> Satisfaction.
> Immortality.

The Encore presents 6 songs that summarize the journey: crossing into spirituality, feeling the connection between Heaven and Earth, being set free with the truth, living love... and feeling fine. This section concludes with "backstage interviews" given by 3 musicians—who open their souls to us.

The Epilogue is my reflection on all of this: looking back, looking up, and looking forward to what shall be... The final 2 songs present a closing musical and spiritual perspective.

The End is Paradise.

The moral of the story of this book: Never say die.

Prologue: The Question

The history of mankind identifies a fascination with prophecies and life in the hereafter. As intelligent life, we have a conscious awareness of our past and present, but do we have a future that extends beyond death? No question on Earth has received more attention. Whether embracing life after death, or accepting no exit from this world, the question remains central to all philosophies and religions. Even if one dismisses the existence of life on the other side, the question of one's real purpose in this life naturally requires an answer. Ironically, an honest pursuit to find one's destiny typically leads straight back to a familiar thought: Why are we here in the first place?

The answer is divided along two lines: Either there is a divine purpose for the Earth or there isn't. We are simply passing through history, or history is being made through us in the form of a greater, supernatural purpose.

Fundamentally, we all seek the obvious: love, belonging, and a sense of worth that satisfies the soul. Whether we are a success or a failure in these vital areas of life is determined by our beliefs. What we believe determines what we become. Our response as intelligent human beings should be only to take great care in determining our personal convictions.

This Prologue sets the stage for the book by introducing 4 musicians who speak of their personal convictions: Alice Cooper, Bono, Brian Wilson, and Justin Hayward.

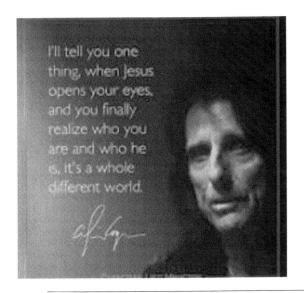

Alice Cooper

In 2011, Mark Lawson—of the BBC (British Broadcasting Corporation)—interviewed Alice Cooper. Cooper said:

"I talk to atheists all the time... [who say] there is no God..., there is no miracles. I say, 'you're looking at a miracle right now.' I was the most addicted alcoholic on the planet. You never saw me without a drink.... Thirty years later, I have never had that craving [to drink]. I really believe God just took it away from me."[1]

In an interview with *Good Morning Britian*, Cooper said, "As far as Christianity goes, for me, I think people have a very strange definition of Christianity. It's really a one-on-one relationship with Jesus Christ."[2]

In the article titled, "'The Real Prodigal Son,' Alice Cooper Shares His Testimony," Cooper states:

"'I grew up in a Christian household,' Cooper told NBC News in 1996. 'My dad was a pastor, and he was an evangelist for 25 years. I used to go up and do missionary work with him with the Apaches in Arizona. My grandfather was a pastor for 75 years... My wife's father is a Baptist pastor, so I always refer to myself as the real prodigal son because I went out and the Lord allowed me to do everything and then just started reeling me back in.'

"'When you get out there you realize that you've had every car, you've had every house and all that, you realize that that's not the answer, that there's a big, big nothing out there at the end of that,' he added. 'Materialism doesn't mean anything. A lot of people say that there's a big God-shaped hole in your heart and when that's filled, then you really are satisfied.... God opens your eyes and it's supernatural. When the Lord opens your eyes, and you suddenly realize who you are and who He is, it's a whole different world.'"3

In the interview titled, "God, Drugs and Rock 'n' Roll: An Interview with Alice Cooper," Pastor Greg Laurie met with Alice Cooper. Excerpts from the interview follow:

"Pastor Laurie: 'Alice, thanks for having me at your place here. It's called The Rock, right?'

"Cooper: 'This is The Rock, yeah, we started it about 20 years ago, trying to find a place for kids to go where they could [have] an alternative to what's on the street, basically.... I watched a couple of 16-yearold kids do a drug deal on the corner, and I went, "how does that kid not know he might be a great guitar player, or that other kid might be a drummer." And it just struck me right then: "Why don't we open that. Give them that alternative to go there"—and it ended up here.'

"Pastor Laurie: 'That's incredible. And I know you're impacting a lot of young people here. And they come in and they wonder what's the catch but you're just doing something for your community.'

"Cooper: 'It's not only that, but it's all Christian. You know, we're all Christian guys and [it's what the] Lord told us to do.'"4

Bono

In the article titled, "Bono on Jesus, C.S. Lewis and King David as a Bluesman," Sarah Bailey writes:

"U2 frontman Bono exchanged Bible references and bantered about music, theology and his role as an AIDS activist in a recent radio interview with Focus on the Family President Jim Daly.

"Growing up in Ireland with a Protestant mother and a Catholic father, Bono imitated C.S. Lewis in Mere Christianity, where Lewis argued that Jesus had to be a lunatic, liar or Lord.

"'When people say, "Good teacher," "Prophet," "Really nice guy," ... this is not how Jesus thought of Himself,' Bono said. 'So, you're left with a challenge in that, which is either Jesus was who He said He was or a complete and utter nut case. And I believe that Jesus was, you know, the Son of God,' Bono said, according to a transcript of the interview. 'I understand that for some people and we need to... be really, really respectful to people who find that ridiculous.'

"In the interview, Bono also made comparisons between Biblical characters and music.

"'First of all, [King] David's a musician so I'm gonna like him,' Bono said. 'What's so powerful about the Psalms are, as well as they're being gospel and songs of praise, they are also the blues. It's very important for Christians to be honest with God, which often, you know, God is much more interested in who you are than who you want to be.'"[5]

The following commentary on Psalm 40 (written by King David) is taken from Bono's book, *Selections from the Book of Psalms*:

"At age of 12, I [Bono] was a fan of [King] David, he felt familiar... like a pop star could feel familiar. The words of the psalms were as poetic as they were religious and he was a star. Years ago, we were still looking for a song to close our third album, *War*. We thought about the psalms. 'Psalm 40' is interesting in that it suggests a time in which grace will replace karma, and love replace the very strict laws of Moses (i.e., fulfill them). I love that thought....

Don't Fear the Reaper

"'40' became the closing song at U2 shows and on hundreds of occasions, literally hundreds of thousands of people of every size and shape t-shirt have shouted back the refrain, pinched from 'Psalm 6': 'How long' (to sing this song)."[6]

40

https://www.youtube.com/watch?v=1XzHlySYR_Y

Brian Wilson & Bono

In an interview with Brian Wilson, the "Professor of Rock" (Adam Reader) talked about The Beach Boys' iconic song, "God Only Knows." And during the interview, Reader quoted Bono. Bono said:

"The GENIUS of his [Brian's] music is the JOY that's in it. I know that Brian believes in angels.

I do too... But you only have to LISTEN to the string arrangement on GOD ONLY KNOWS for fact and proof of angels."[7]

God Only Knows

https://www.youtube.com/watch?v=NTrvttaDwJM

Brian Wilson

"I believe that God is music.... So when you make music, that's God talking to you."[8]

Brian Wilson spoke of God communicating through music.

Bono spoke of his belief in angels, and of his personal conviction: Jesus of Nazareth is the Son of God.

Alice Cooper spoke of his addiction to alcohol. Yet, he didn't succumb to the alcoholic vapors of selfoblivion; he embraced a new habit: spirituality via Christ. His freedom began. And Alice Cooper isn't alone regarding being set free.

Justin Hayward

"Question"

What is it to seek a miracle that Justin Hayward—of The Moody Blues—cried out for in the song "Question"? Enlightenment.

In 2006, Justin Hayward gave an interview for "The Word":

"Hayward: 'I felt I was speaking for a lot of other people in the late '60s. I wanted to write about our search for enlightenment, as simple as that. I'm still kind of doing it.'

"Interviewer: 'And where has this search brought Justin Hayward in 2006?'

"Hayward: 'I would have to say Christianity,' he answers. 'I came from a family with a very strong faith, I moved away through all sorts of Eastern religions, through meditation, the Tibetan Book of the Dead, anything else. It was reading C.S Lewis, books like Mere Christianity, that helped me to define what I really felt and finally decide. So I came full circle.'"[9]

Moody Blues – Question

https://www.youtube.com/watch?v=-wDHvmCVRxU

In the pages that follow, the songs* reflect the purpose of this book: to hitch a ride on a journey with musical artists who travel across the landscape of life and reveal what they see.

*Scanning the QR code will open the YouTube webpage link to the song. To scan the QR code, use your phone's camera (as if you were going to take a photo). Center the QR code on the screen. You will need to hold it for a few seconds, and a link will appear on the screen (at the top, or bottom, or right below the QR code). Tap the link to open the webpage.

1. https://www.youtube.com/watch?v=E7j4vcRoho k&t=614s.   Retrieval date: Oct. 2, 2023.

2. https://www.youtube.com/results?search_query =alice+cooper+interview+british. Retrieval date: August 24, 2023.

3. https://www.movieguide.org/news-articles/thereal-prodigal-son-alice-cooper-shares-histestimony.html. Retrieval date: July 12, 2023.

4. https://www.youtube.com/results?search_query =Pastor+Greg+Laurie+God%2C+Drugs+and+Rock+%E2%80%98n%E2%80%99+Roll%3A+An+I nterview+with+Alice+Cooper. Retrieval date: June 30, 2023.

5. https://thinkchristian.net/bono-on-jesus-cslewis-and-king-david-as-a-bluesman. Retrieval date: July 11, 2023.

6. https://*Selections from the Book of Psalms*, (New York: Grove Press, 1999), vii, xi.

7. https://www.youtube.com/watch?v=gV62RewgC WM. Retrieval date: November 26, 2023.

8. **https://www.youtube.com/watch?v=gV62R ewgC WM. Retrieval date: November 26, 2023.**
9. **https://www.pauldunoyer.com/moody-bluesinterview/. Retrieval date: May 23, 2024.**

ACT ONE

William Ayles, D.D.

1 All You Need is Love

The summer of 1967 is forever known as the "Summer of Love."

And the Summer of Love is forever connected to "All You Need is Love"—which The Beatles sang live in London before millions of people around the globe via satellite on June 25, 1967.

As found in the 2020 article, "Flashback: The Beatles Perform 'All You Need is Love' Via Global Satellite":

"It was 53 years ago today (June 25, 1967) that The Beatles performed 'All You Need Is Love,' which was broadcast live via global satellite to an estimated 400 million viewers. The Beatles were representing the U.K. in the *Our World*

TV special, which was the first major televised hookup linking five continents....

Over the years, the song has become synonymous with 1967's legendary Summer Of Love.

"The Beatles, who sat on high stools in Abbey Road Studio Number One, were decked out in their finest Swinging London apparel, with John Lennon, who composed the song, sitting center stage without an instrument.

"'All You Need Is Love', along with the Beatles' other two Number One's from that year, 'Penny Lane' and 'Hello Goodbye,' was included on the soundtrack album to the group's *Magical Mystery Tour* album, which was released that December [1967]. A colorized version of the Beatles' performance of 'All You Need Is Love' was included in the 1995 *Beatles Anthology*.

"In *The Beatles Anthology* book, Ringo Starr commented on the altruistic aspects of the Beatles performing 'All You Need Is Love' on a truly global stage: 'We were big enough to command an audience of that size, and it was for love. It was for love and bloody peace. It was a fabulous time. I even get excited now when I realize that's what it was for: peace and love, people putting flowers in guns.'

"George Harrison recalled the recording of the song in 1995's *The Beatles Anthology*: ['I don't know how many millions of people but it was supposed to be some phenomenal amount of people and it was probably the very earliest technology that enabled that kind of satellite link. We just thought, "Well, we'll just sing 'All You Need Is Love,' because it's a kind of subtle bit of PR for God," (*laughs*) basically.']"[1]

Paul said, "We had been told we'd be seen recording it by the whole world at the same time. So we had one message for the world—Love. We need more love in the world."[2]

And John said, "I think if you get down to basics, whatever the problem is it's usually to do with love. So I think 'All You Need is Love' is a true statement."[3]

ALL YOU NEED IS LOVE

Songwriters: John Lennon / Paul McCartney
Performed by The Beatles
https://www.youtube.com/watch?v=_paPrwogAUo

Related Thoughts

In the article titled, "Did John Lennon have a 'God Complex'?" Drew Wardle writes:

"While he [John Lennon] had strong feelings towards the idea of Jesus Christ and the Buddha as spiritual leaders, he never quite liked the idea of religion as an institutionalized idea. This Lennon remark can perhaps elucidate the issue a bit:

"'I'm one of Christ's biggest fans. And if I can turn the focus on the Beatles on to Christ's message, then that's what we're here to do.... People always got the image I was an anti-Christ or antireligion. I'm not. I'm a most religious fellow.'"[4]

In the article titled, "What John Lennon Said About Jesus Just Before He Died," Matthew Trzcinski writes:

"John said he wasn't 'anti-Christian.' He believed the good things people said about Jesus. He said his comment that The Beatles were 'more popular than Jesus' was made offhand, and he wasn't trying to say the Fab Four were superior to Christ.

"John then promoted individual religious figures. 'Read Christ's words, read Buddha's words, any of the great words,' he said.

"John explained what religion meant to him. 'I'm religious in the sense of [admitting there is] more to it than meets the eye,' he revealed. 'I'm certainly not an atheist. There is more that we still could know.'

"John created controversy with his remarks about Jesus, but near the end of his life he asked his fans to read Christ's words."[5]

In the article titled, "Paul McCartney: Beatles' 'more popular than Jesus' remark was 'pro-religion,'" Josh Saunders writes:

"In 1966, he [Lennon] made a comment to *The Evening Standard* about the band being 'more popular than Jesus'. Sir Paul said: 'The John thing got to us and mainly got to him because it was taken out of context. He was actually saying some quite positive, optimistic stuff.' John's slip of the tongue came after he was asked about 'the popularity of The Beatles'.

"Sir Paul recalled: 'He [Lennon] was saying, "You know, the thing is, all the churches these days are empty. No one is going to church, like when we were kids people went to church". But in his point that "No one was really going to church", he said "You know, we get more people at our concerts than ever go to church". He said, "In fact, we're more popular than Jesus".'

'"It was just a throwaway remark, referring to the fact that it was a pity that people didn't go to church and [were] losing that social aspect. He [Lennon] had an answer for it, which was that he was actually being positive about religion.'

"He [Lennon] said: 'I suppose if I had said, "Television was more popular than Jesus", I would have got away with it. I'm sorry I opened my mouth – I'm not anti-God, anti-Christ or anti-religion. I was not knocking it, I was not saying we are greater or better.'

"SIR PAUL MCCARTNEY claimed John Lennon's famous quote that The Beatles were 'more popular than Jesus' was misinterpreted and was actually part of a pro-religious statement."6

In the article titled, "'No one was Saved' Paul McCartney out-harshed Lennon's Critique with 4 words," Elizabeth Scalia quoted Paul McCartney speaking about the song "Eleanor Rigby." Paul said:

"The Church is failing in its mission to save; it is becoming irrelevant to people's lives because it is too self-concerned, too insular, too busy protecting its own interests — darning its socks — while the world spins and the pews empty, and humanity grows ever more lonely, more isolated, and social interaction becomes more fleeting, more guarded and inauthentic (wearing faces kept handy by the door...or the twitter Facebook feed) until it disappears completely, and no one is saved."[7]

In the article titled, "John Lennon Revealed 'Imagine' Wasn't Actually an Attack on Religion," Matthew Trzcinski writes:

"In one line of the song [Imagine], John famously asks his fans to imagine a world with 'no religion.' John elaborated on this lyric: 'If you can imagine a world at peace, with no denominations of religion — not without religion but without this my-God-is-bigger-than-your-God thing — then it can be true,' he opined."[8]

Lennon said:

"Studying religion has made me try to improve relationships, not to be unpleasant. It's not a conscious move to change my personality. I'm just trying to be how I want to be, and how I'd like others to be."[9]

"I don't profess to be a practicing Christian, and Christ was what he was, and anything anybody says great about him I believe."[10]

"I was brought up a Christian and I only now understand some of the things that Christ was saying in those parables."[11]

GIMME SOME TRUTH

Released in 1971, the *Imagine* album included the song, "Gimme Some Truth."[12]

Regarding truth, Lennon once said:

"The thing about rock & roll, good rock & roll… is that it's real, and realism gets through to you…. You recognize something in it which is true…. If it's real, it's simple, usually; and if it's simple, it's true."[13]

https://www.youtube.com/watch?v=X1GOF4G_Qj8

"In a 2012 interview with **The Independent [UK Newspaper]**, Paul [McCartney] discussed his religious beliefs and whether or not he subscribed to a particular **faith journey**. He said, 'Not really. I have personal faith in something good, but it doesn't go much further than that. It's certainly not subscribing to any organized religion.'

"He continued, 'I think that [organized religion] is the cause of a lot of trouble – "My God is better than yours." But I think there is something greater than me, and that's not easy to imagine.'"[14]

Hope For the Future

In the 2014 article titled, "Sir Paul McCartney interview: 'New song is a manifesto for the future'," Lewis Corner quoted McCartney:

"I wrote this track that would be hopeful because the idea of the game is to save mankind. The song would be, 'What are we going to achieve? What are we going to do in the future that's out there?' I wanted it to be anthemic and our manifesto for the future."[15]

Paul wrote the song for commercial purposes. Yet, the lyrics align with spirituality and prophecy—which is why it's in this chapter. It is an inspired work. A masterpiece.

https://www.youtube.com/watch?v=163_C5U VU-I

In an interview, Ringo Starr was asked about God, the afterlife, and "peace and love."

"Interviewer: 'What is God?'"

"Ringo: 'God to me? My God in my life: God is love, pure love.'"

"'Love is an incredible power. You know if you give out love the reaction to it is so great even to crazy violent people. If you give out love, they stop for a minute because everybody notices love when it's coming your way. You know and you feel incredible when you give love back.'"

"'I feel that as you go through life you make certain moves. And it's very hard these moves. And you don't feel good about it, but if you're doing something with love, all of this behind you, all over the world will support you. So that's how it is. That's how the world works. It's all the one God.'

"Interviewer: 'What do you think happens when you die?'

"Ringo: 'Personally I believe I go somewhere.'

"Interviewer: 'So you believe that your spirit is separate from your body?'

"Ringo: 'I do.'

"Interviewer: 'Some people who ran into the "peace and love" message in the 1960s gave up on it. How did you hold onto the "peace and love" Ringo?'

"Ringo: 'It just became natural for greeting: "peace and love" brother.'"[16]

OCTOPUS'S GARDEN

In a 1969 interview, George Harrison said:

"'Octopus's Garden' is Ringo's song. It's only the second song Ringo wrote, and it's lovely. Ringo gets bored playing the drums, and at home he plays a bit of piano, but he only knows about three chords. He knows about the same on guitar. I think it's a really great song, because on the surface, ... [it's] just like a daft kids' song, but the lyrics are great. For me, you know, I find very deep meaning in the lyrics, which Ringo probably doesn't see, but all the things like 'resting our head on the sea bed' and 'We'll be warm beneath the storm' which is really great, you know. Because it's like this level is a storm, and if you get sort of deep in your consciousness, it's very peaceful. So Ringo's writing his cosmic songs without noticing."17

https://www.youtube.com/watch?v=V-BdGchSoyk

My Sweet Lord

In the article titled, "George Harrison: 'My Sweet Lord,'" Ralph Burden writes:

"Close friends have revealed that George was a seeker of Christ for some time before he met [Dr.] Louis Palou [International Evangelist who gave George a Christian Devotional, 'Daily Bread'].

"Although always a fan of Christ the teacher, it appears that in his final year he [George] also embraced Jesus Christ as the one he claimed to be, God the Son, the Saviour of all people who turn to him. In the Bible, God states,

"'Those who seek me will find me.' (Jeremiah 29:13, Proverbs 8:17, Luke 11:10)

"The media representation of George is generally of a spiritual seeker who embraced Eastern Mysticism. This was only a part of his journey. It seems that all along he was seeking the One True God rather than just a 'religious experience,' and George found him in the person of Jesus Christ in the final months of his life on earth.

"George's wife Olivia said that the last words George spoke before he died were the words of Jesus recorded in John 13:34, 'Love one another.'

"George's awesome single 'My Sweet Lord' was originally written in praise of the Hindu God Krishna. It reached number one on singles charts globally in 1971. After his Christian conversion, George changed the emphasis. He told the evangelist who prayed with him that he was re-dedicating the song to Jesus Christ. Following George's death in November 2001, the song was re-released and topped the charts again in 2002. This time it was in praise of Jesus Christ, God the Son, the Saviour of the World!"[18]

https://www.youtube.com/watch?v=VHc6COM-Y6o

George Harrison searched—and found.

Christ asked us... to seek and find:

"Ask and it will be given to you; seek and you will find; knock and the door will be opened to you. For everyone who asks receives; the one who seeks finds; and to the one who knocks, the door will be opened. Which of you fathers, if your son asks for a fish, will give him a snake instead? Or if he asks for an egg, will give him a scorpion? If you then, though you are evil, know how to give good gifts to your children, how much more will your Father in heaven give the Holy Spirit [the Spirit of Truth] to those who ask him!"[19]

1. https://nightswithalicecooper.com/2020/06/25/fl   ashback-the-beatles-perform-all-

you-need-is-lovelive-via-global-satellite/). Retrieval date: July 12, 2023.
2. https://www.beatlesinterviews.org/db67.html. Retrieval date: August 21, 2023.
3. https://www.youtube.com/watch?v=IwfzqgYaAvc. Retrieval date: September 3, 2023.
4. https://faroutmagazine.co.uk/did-john-lennonsuffer-from-a-god-complex/. Retrieval date: July 12, 2023.
5. https://www.cheatsheet.com/entertainment/john-lennon-said-jesus-just-died.html/. Retrieval date: July 12, 2023.
6. https://www.express.co.uk/entertainment/music/1396536/paul-mccartney-news-the-beatles-johnlennon-music-jesus-religion-christian-spt. Retrieval date: July 13, 2023.
7. https://theanchoress.com/no-one-was-saved-paulmccartney-out-harshed-lennons-critique-with-4-words/. Retrieval date: May 23, 2024.
8. https://www.cheatsheet.com/entertainment/john-lennon-revealed-imagine-wasnt-attackreligion.html/. Retrieval date: August 21, 2023.
9. https://www.beatlesinterviews.org/db67.html.
Retrieval date: August 21, 2023.
10. https://www.cheatsheet.com/entertainment/john-lennon-discussed-jesus-react-the-beatleseleanor-rigby.html/. Retrieval date: October 20, 2023.
11. https://tittenhurstlennon.blogspot.com/2009/08/john-lennon-in-new-york-city-8th-

28th_8807.html. Retrieval date: May 24, 2024.
12. https://www.johnlennon.com. Retrieval date: February 21, 2024.
13. https://www.rollingstone.com/music/musicnews/lennon-rembered-gimme-some-truth77285/. Retrieval date: February 21, 2024.
14. https://www.cheatsheet.com/entertainment/paulmccartney-fantasized-faith-filled-truck-driver.html/. Retrieval date: May 24, 2024.
15. https://www.digitalspy.com/music/a614725/sir-paulmccartney-interview-new-song-is-a-manifesto-for-thefuture/. Retrieval date: May 24, 2024.
16. https://www.youtube.com/watch?v=JKh1IozcHY4. Retrieval date: May 22, 2024.
17. https://www.beatlesbible.com/songs/octopuss-garden/. Retrieval date: June 1, 2024.
18. https://www.reallifestories.org/stories/george-harrisonmy-sweet-lord/. Retrieval date: May 23, 2024.
19. Luke 11:9–13.

2
Break On Through (To the Other Side)

In the article titled, "The Doors, Break On Through: the meaning of Jim Morrison's visions," Dario Giardi writes:

"Crossing the prophetic 'doors of perception', as predicted by William Blake, was becoming the only way to escape from this dirty, corrupt, agonizing world. At least, this was possible with our minds. The desire to escape from reality hides a deep need to know. We are fascinated by the unknown and we keep asking ourselves questions like, 'What is the meaning of life?' 'What comes after death?' 'Are we alone in the universe?'

"The thing we all are most hungry for is knowledge. It's knowing what the meaning of life is, and it's precisely what science has never been able to provide. Only religion has been able to partly fill this void. And we all continue to seek a 'sense' of our existence.

"That's why Break On Through, the song that summarizes Morrison's visionary poetics in the best possible way, is an exhortation, an imperative: open the passage to the other side.

"The world is the kingdom of illusions and contraries ("You know the day destroys the night / Night divides the day"), the place that tries to stop our research.... What we need is clear: we have to open up the pathway and reach the other side. The side of 'life' where you see things as they really are.

"The answers that Jim Morrison gives are therefore uncertain and enigmatic.... What is certain, however, is that one cannot help but continue to seek balance amid so much chaos, otherwise living will always be like being carried away on an unstoppable tide."[1]

Break On Through (To the Other Side)

Songwriters: Jim Morrison / John Densmore / Ray Manzarek / Robbie Krieger
Performed by The Doors
https://www.youtube.com/watch?v=j2QsppODuiw

Related Thoughts

Jim Morrison said, "There are different kinds of freedom – there's a lot of misunderstanding.... The most important kind of freedom is to be what you really are. You trade in your reality for a role. You trade in your senses for an act. You give up your ability to feel, and in exchange, put on a mask. There can't be any large-scale revolution until there's a personal revolution, on an individual level. It's got to happen inside first."[2]

LIGHT MY FIRE

In 1967, The Doors released their first album, and it featured their hit, "Light My Fire." This song takes on an intriguing picture when viewed through the eyes of band member Ray Manzarek. Manzarek stated:

"My God, 'Light my Fire' had the magic in it. Robby [Krieger] was blessed, just like how in the Bible the Holy Ghost comes and blesses Jesus' disciples and a little tongue of flame descends upon all their heads. A tongue of flame descended upon Robby's head when he wrote 'LIGHT MY FIRE.'"[3]

William Ayles, D.D.

https://www.youtube.com/watch?v=aKd6yarfkxA

WHEN THE MUSIC'S OVER

In 1967, The Doors released their second album, Strange Days—which included the song, "When the Music's Over." In that song, Jim Morrison sang about Jesus saving us.

https://www.youtube.com/watch?v=CKw9JA66H-A

When "The Doors of the 21st Century" performed in Connecticut in 2003, I was in the audience. During the show, I heard the keyboard player, Ray Manzarek, say something profound about our Creator—and us. He said:

"God bless you all.... We're all here together. It's all one people. It's all one love. God made every single person here—everything here. Let's worship the Creator.... It's all one energy, flowing out of the energy into me, into you. You send it back to us, we send it back to you. And maybe, maybe by the grace of God we can save the world and make it a better place to live and to love."[4]

And during the show, when the lead singer—Ian Astbury—sang "When the Music's Over," he sang about Jesus saving us.

In the 2022 article titled, "New Memoir by The Doors' Robby Krieger Sets the Record Straight," Brian Fishbach writes:

"Krieger's book is one of the most entertaining music memoirs in recent years. He is just as sharp at writing on paper as he is at working the fretboard. 'Set the Night on Fire' is an enjoyable, witty and fast-paced 400-page greatest hits album of memories and reflection of a life and career well-lived. He was born Jewish, yet he reflects on his existence as one of music's most revered guitarists with a non-denominational spirituality, positivity and gratitude."[5]

In the 2020 *Rolling Stone* article titled, "The Doors' John Densmore on His Eternal Music and Spiritual Bond With Ray Manzarek," Jon Blistein quoted Densmore:

"I'm starting to worry that I now sound like my devoted Catholic mother, who is 'gonna see all her friends in Heaven.' I don't *see* things quite that literally. I feel that when the body passes, the spirit continues, but in what form that energy manifests I haven't a clue. It's a mystery to me ... a great mystery. That's why when asked if I believe in God, I answer, 'I believe in the Mystery, with a capital M.'"6

"Break On Through (To the Other Side)"

Morrison sang about crossing into another dimension of knowledge…

And Christ spoke about crossing into another dimension of knowledge—which unfolds in this book. He revealed what we need to know about the spiritual realm—including the kingdom of God:

> "The kingdom of God does not come with your careful observation… because the kingdom of God is within you."7

In the article titled, "The Doors 'Break On Through,'" Jeff Weiss writes:

"The Doors now occupy a similar space as their hero, Kerouac, and his hero, Dean Moriarty — Western kinsmen of the sun…. [The Doors] serve as a gateway to a world of influences, from French surrealism to the sweltering Chicago blues, from the modal genius of John Coltrane to German expressionism, from Sophocles to William Blake. They exist to get you to the starting point, and wherever the path diverges from there is on you."8

1. https://auralcrave.com/en/2018/06/24/the doors-break-on-through-jim-morrisons-

2. https://www.patrickwanis.com/jim-morrisonfreedom-lizzie-james-interview/. Retrieval date: August 19, 2023.
3. Alan Paul, "The Doors of Perception," *Revolver,* Premiere Issue, p. 75.
4. https://www.youtube.com/results?search_query= The+Doors+of+the+21st+Century+-+Live+%40Oakdale+Theatre. Retrieval date: September 29, 2023.
5. https://jewishjournal.com/culture/arts/books/34 3781/new-memoir-by-the-doors-robby-kriegersets-the-record-straight/. Retrieval date: May 24, 2024.
6. https://www.rollingstone.com/music/musicnews/the-doors-john-densmore-seekers-book1089389/. Retrieval date: May 24, 2024.
7. Luke 17:20, 21.
8. https://www.vinylmeplease.com/blogs/magazine/thedoors-liner-notes. Retrieval date: August 19, 2023.

3   Turn! Turn! Turn!

In the article titled, "Pete Seeger's Greatest Hits — Turn Turn Turn," Stephen Pate writes:

"With words from the Book of Ecclesiastes [from the Old Testament], Pete Seeger wrote a timeless song that became a #1 hit for The Byrds in 1965."[1]

"'Turn! Turn! Turn!' is based on the Book of Ecclesiastes 3:1–8. Seeger explained why he based the track on that passage. 'I was leafing through it when I came on that poem,' he recalled. 'I just leafed through it by chance. Maybe God led me to it. Who knows?'"[2]

In the article titled, "Earliest Known Recording of Folk Classic 'Turn! Turn! Turn!' Surfaces (Exclusive)," Mitch Myers writes:

"[Roger] McGuinn and The Byrds had intuitively tapped into the deeper folk traditions of Pete Seeger for a unifying song of meaning. Amidst the tumult over the Vietnam War, rising social and racial protest and the emergence of flower power, it was a message of change, hope and acceptance, drawn from the Bible itself — a song that came to characterize the blossoming of the 1960s. A song whose time had come, as it was the season."³

In the article titled, "Turn! Turn! Turn! — The Byrds' 1965 hit used lyrics that dated back more than 2,000 years," Nick Keppler writes:

"The song reached number one in the US in December 1965. A chorus of shaggy-haired young men [The Byrds] pressed the nation to 'turn, turn, turn' and accept that change is inevitable, history is a cycle, strife is temporary, and to everything there is a season.

"The words attributed 'a season' to a series of opposing actions: 'A time to be born, a time to die; a time to plant, a time to reap; a time to kill, a time to heal,' etc. Seeger took the text almost verbatim. He added the 'turn, turn, turn' to build a chorus and tacked on his own hopeful concluding line for cold war audiences: 'A time of peace; I swear it's not too late.'"⁴

TURN! TURN! TURN!

Songwriter: Peter Seeger

Performed by The Byrds
https://www.youtube.com/watch?v=W3xgcmIS3YU

Related Thoughts

Roger McGuinn's friend, Camilla (now his wife), recounted when she first met Roger in an acting class (in 1978). In that class, Roger sang to her. And, in a blog about this experience, Camilla wrote the following:

"He [Roger] had sung 'I like the Christian Life,' a song the BYRDS recorded on 'Sweetheart of the Rodeo.' Then I [Camilla] figured out what he was up to. He was going to try to tell me about Jesus on stage, in front of a class! I asked him sarcastically, 'How long have you been into Jesus?' 'A few months.'"[5]

Check out McGuinn's website: www.mcguinn.com. Roger has toured the country, playing his extensive collection of enduring songs.

Byrds' band member David Crosby posted about Roger McGuinn and another band member Chris Hillman:

"There is nothing wrong or even weird about Roger and for that matter Chris either …being Christians… they both try to walk the walk not just talk about it…. that's fine with me. They are trying to be decent human beings. We are on the same side."[6]

"Turn! Turn! Turn!"

"Turn! Turn! Turn!" holds a unique place in rock history: It is the oldest #1 hit, because (most of) the lyrics come to us from the Book of Ecclesiastes.

This book was written by King Solomon (who reigned as king of Israel around 950 BC).[7] In his book, Solomon reflected on his life—and revealed an astounding truth: Our Creator handed us the key to unlock the mystery of life; He placed eternity in our hearts. Each one of us is designed by our Creator to seek eternity (eternal life). This is what Solomon recorded:

> "He [God] has made everything beautiful in its time. He has also set eternity in the human heart; yet no one can fathom what God has done from beginning to end."[8]

Solomon then concluded the matter by referring to our life in this world: Since life is comprised of various (limited) seasons, let our response be... all in. Solomon said:

> "I experienced that there is nothing better for them than to be glad and do good in their life. And also that everyone should eat and drink and experience good in all their labor. This is a gift of God. I have perceived that everything that God has done will be lasting."[9]

And Christ added to the wisdom of Solomon:

"I came that they [we] may have and enjoy life, and have it in abundance (to the full, till it overflows)."[10]

1. https://njnnetwork.com/2012/03/pete-seegersgreatest-hits-turn-turn-turn/. Retrieval date:

September 6, 2023.
2. https://www.cheatsheet.com/entertainment/th e-byrds-turn-turn-turn-based-1-passagebible.html/. Retrieval date: July 12, 2023.
3. https://variety.com/2018/music/news/turn turn-turn-earliest-recording-pete-seeger-demo-1202913433/. Retrieval date: September 6, 2023.
4. https://ig.ft.com/life-of-a-song/turn-turnturn.html#:~:text=But%20the%20song%20itself%20was,a%20letter%20from%20his%20publisher. Retrieval date: August 21, 2023.
5. https://rogermcguinn.blogspot.com/2023/. Retrieval date: December 2, 2023.
6. https://x.com/thedavidcrosby/status/1110010090 994581504. Retrieval date: May 28, 2024.
7. Ecclesiastes 1:1 states: "The words of the Teacher, son of David, king of Jerusalem." Rabbinic tradition holds to the belief that King Solomon wrote this book.
8. Ecclesiastes 3:11.
9. Ecclesiastes 3:12–14.
10. John 10:10, *Amplified, Classic Edition.*

4 The Sound of Silence

As found in *The Allen Ginsberg Project*, Paul Simon commented on the origin of "The Sound of Silence":

"Whatever your creative process is it comes through you and it's yours but it's almost like you didn't write it. I didn't know at that point, because I was twenty-two years old, that such a thing could happen. As years passed I began to recognize that that was an unusual and inspirational kind of occurrence."[1]

William Ayles, D.D.

In the article titled, "The Profound Meaning of Simon & Garfunkel's 'The Sound of Silence,'" Alli Patton writes:

"[Paul Simon] chalks up the song's popularity to its simple sing-ability, the song resonates with a number of people who have ever felt alienated and disassociated from their present society. What lives at the heart of the tune's existential poetry is the collectively relatable feeling.

"[Simon stated] 'Really the key to "The Sound of Silence" is the simplicity of the melody and the words, which are youthful alienation. It wasn't something that I [Simon] was experiencing at some deep, profound level – nobody's listening to me, nobody's listening to anyone – it was a post-adolescent angst,' Simon continued, 'but it had some level of truth to it and it resonated with millions of people.'

"[Patton writes] While it's easy to get swept up in the tune's haunting monotone and wispy melody – the perfect tune to set a dramatic scene – it's easier to miss the song's moral entirely. Now more than ever, 'The Sound of Silence' is worth a revisit and a real honest listen.

"[In 'The Sound of Silence'] The narrator [Simon] has no one to talk to and the only thing that understands him is the darkness and his own loneliness. *In restless dreams I walked alone / Narrow streets of cobblestone.* But the song reaches beyond the perspective of a single narrator, a flash of light revealing a mass of people, humanity all seeking refuge in their own darkness and their own silence. The chilling verse plays, illustrating a near, all-tooreal future in which interactions become all the more surface-level and indifference continues to grow.... [T]he duo [Simon & Garfunkel] sings a wake-up call to no avail.

"'The Sound of Silence' comes to a close with a warning, pointedly calling out the all-consuming consumerism and using those already lost to it as an example of what's to come if we continue to find solace in silence."[2]

THE SOUND OF SILENCE

Songwriter: Paul Simon
Performed by Simon & Garfunkel
https://www.youtube.com/watch?v=JOPNVdl6GRY

William Ayles, D.D.

Related Thoughts

"The Sound of Silence"

In the 2016 article titled, "David Draiman Talks 'The Sound of Silence,' Returning to Touring + More," Chad Childers writes:

"Disturbed made their triumphant return last year with the release of the Immortalized album and they're currently selling out shows and topping the charts with their cover of Simon & Garfunkel's 'The Sound of Silence.' We recently had a chance to speak with Disturbed's David Draiman to get the lowdown on the band's return to touring, the creation of their cover of 'The Sound of Silence' and his thoughts on some of the band's upcoming festival appearances.

"'The lyrics always spoke to me ever since I [Draiman] was first exposed to it as a child…. If you listen to the intricacy of the lyric it's talking about someone who is enveloped in the darkness, who welcomes it, who feels like he is a bit of an outcast in a world full of chaos, who feels like someone who's an introvert in a world full of extroverts, who feels like someone who's bearing witness to things that they can't come to terms with and who's trying to express words that fall on fears and unfortunately wisdom that doesn't end up getting developed. Tremendously poignant.'"3

Art Garfunkel was interviewed by The Jewish Chronicle for the article titled, "Art Garfunkel: The truth about me and Paul."

"Garfunkel: 'I like to think I sing for the universal spirit. I'm not in favour of identifying with religious differences.... I sing for anybody with a heart and sense of beauty.'

"Interviewer: 'His [Garfunkel's] all-embracing attitude has served him well. Like those other Jewish musicians who became household names in the '60s and '70s - including Bob Dylan, Leonard Cohen, Lou Reed and, of course, Paul Simon - Garfunkel spoke to a generation, irrespective of their creed. He's a singer first, and a Jew second.'"4

SEVEN PSALMS

In 2023, Paul Simon released his latest production: *Seven Psalms*.

In *The New Yorker* magazine article titled, "The beautiful mystery of Paul Simon's 'Seven Psalms,'" Amanda Petrusich writes:

"*Seven Psalms* is focused on a more expansive, open ended notion of God. Simon has described the piece as 'argument I'm having with myself about belief—or not.'"5

What follows are excerpts from an article in PremierChristianity.com on *Seven Psalms*:

"The 81-year-old's latest project sees him musing on God, forgiveness and his own mortality. Paul Simon's new release *Seven Psalms* is so blatantly spiritual that it has turned a few heads, but scratch under the surface of his music and you find that he has been pondering deeper things for years.

"*Christianity Today* magazine noted that his 2011 album *So Beautiful or So What* made several best-of-year lists, including their own. One of their headlines the next year was Simon admitting, 'God comes up a lot in my songs.' Only four years ago, in an NBC interview, he said, 'You get to a point where you have a mastery over what you're doing; then you say, What is it that I'm supposed to do with the time I have left?' *Seven Psalms* – both its intense lyrics and the way the release came about – has revealed some of the answer to that question.

"HOW IT CAME ABOUT

"We often hear of artists telling us that the music was 'given' to them, but Simon is very specific about how and when this one was telegraphed through.

"In the trailer for *Seven Psalms*, he tells how in January 2019, 'I had a dream that said, "You're working on a piece called *Seven Psalms*." The dream was so strong that I got up and wrote it down, but I had no idea what that meant. Gradually, information would come. I would start to wake up two or three times a week between 3:30 and 5 in the morning, and words would come. I'd write them down and start to put them together.'

"He even shows the notepaper he first used and the time he woke from the dream that fed him the words (1:59am). The sheet is now framed on his office wall.

"Simon wasn't even sure what a psalm was, so had to go to the Bible to check it out. And between the initial advice that he would write his piece and getting those night-time phrases, he spent a year working on little guitar pieces.

"WHAT IT IS – AND ISN'T

"Simon insists that this is not a collection of seven songs, but a single piece of acoustic music to be heard all the way through. Despite seven headings, the first psalm, with its more discernible tune, reprises a few times throughout the work. It is the flexible spine of this meandering ragtag collection of phrases.

'"THIS WHOLE THING IS REALLY AN ARGUMENT I'M HAVING WITH MYSELF ABOUT BELIEF'

"Questions, contradictions and ponderings are sprinkled across the lyric sheet, some visible, some implied.

"WHAT ABOUT GOD?

"In this release, his notion of God is largely Christian. Underlying his understanding of death and afterlife are gospel concepts ('And I the last in the line / Hoping the gates won't be closed before your forgiveness') and regular references to 'The Lord' underline his specific suspicion of who gives him these dreams.

"From the Old Testament, Simon sings of 'The sacred harp / That David played to make his songs of praise' and there is direct reference to the incarnation when he sings, 'Go carry my grievances down to the shore / Wash'em away in the tumbling tide… all that really matters is the one who became us / Anointed and gained us with his opinion.'

"LIFE AND DEATH

"Simon is clearly wrestling here. It's hard to know which influence is stronger: the direct gift of the dream and words, or the increasingly acute awareness of his mortality. Either way, it seems he wants answers.

"'I've been thinking about our troubled nature / Our benediction and our curse / Are we all just trial and error / One of a billion in the universe?' and later, 'I have my reasons to doubt... Two billion heartbeats and out / Or does it all begin again?'

"As the work comes to a close ('Wait'), he focuses on what is to come, although desperately pleading for more time. 'I want to believe in a dreamless transition... I don't want to be near my dark intuition / I need you here by my side / My beautiful mystery guide / Wait / Life is a meteor... Heaven is beautiful / It's almost like home / Children get ready / It's time to come home. Amen.'

"Amen indeed." [6]

I admire Paul Simon's transparency. First, he acknowledges a source of inspiration that opens a door in his mind—which he turns into a musical expression. Second, he acknowledges his personal conflict with belief: It remains unresolved.

William Ayles, D.D.

I think we all can take a lesson from Simon regarding his transparency. Looking back on my life, I can say some of the greatest moments came from simply being vulnerable—transparent. Especially because transparency set the stage for my embrace of eternity.

And like Simon, some of my greatest moments have also come by way of dreams… A few years ago, while sound asleep at 3:00 a.m., I heard a voice in my head that said, "What really matters?" Then I heard, "At the end of the day, how do you feel about that?" At that moment, I heard a doorbell ring. I woke up, shot out of bed, and looked out the window. No one was there. It was a wakeup call… Seize the day!

"The Sound of Silence"

Simon sings of solace found in darkness. And in that "darkness," he encounters a stabbing "light." He then perceives what no one else seems to perceive: reality for what it truly is. Tragically, his attempt to reach those in their own darkness of silence… falls on deaf ears.

Jesus issued a strikingly similar statement—referring to those in His day, blinded by their own "darkness":

> "By hearing, you will hear and shall not understand, and seeing, you will see and shall not perceive; for this people's heart has grown dull. Their ears have

become hard of hearing, and they have closed their eyes, lest they should see with their eyes and hear with their ears and understand with their hearts, and turn, and I should heal them."[7]

1. https://allenginsberg.org/2021/10/w-o-13/. Retrieval date: July 15, 2023.
2. https://americansongwriter.com/the-profoundmeaning-behind-simon-garfunkels-the-sound-ofsilence/. Retrieval date: July 15, 2023.
3. https://loudwire.com/disturbed-david-draimanthe-sound-of-silence-touring-more/. Retrieval date: July 16, 2023.
4. https://www.thejc.com/life-and-culture/artgarfunkel-the-truth-about-me-and-paulv5rmy8hf. Retrieval date: June 1, 2024.
5. *The New Yorker*, The Music Issue, (June 5, 2023), p. 80.
6. https://www.premierchristianity.com/reviews/sev en-psalms-paul-simons-latest-album-is-blatantlyspiritual/15665.article. Retrieval date: July 11, 2023.
7. Matthew 13:14, 15.

William Ayles, D.D.

5 Carry On Wayward Son

In the article titled, "The story behind the song: Carry On Wayward Son by Kansas," Dave Ling writes:

"In keeping with the group's strong religious beliefs, the guitarist [Kerry Livgren] still suspects that a helping hand from above may have played a part in the song's meaning. 'It's an autobiographical song,' he explains. 'Parallel to my musical career I've always been on a spiritual sojourn, looking for truth and meaning. It was a song of self-encouragement. I was telling myself to keep on looking and I would find what I sought.'"[1]

In the article titled, "The Story Behind the Autobiographical Kansas Hit 'Carry On Wayward Son,'" Tina Benitez-Eves writes:

"Just two days before the band was set to record *Leftoverture*, Livgren had one last song to present, 'Carry On Wayward Son.' Once released, 'Carry On Wayward Son' became the band's first major hit and skyrocketed them into stardom.

"[With 'Carry On Wayward Son'] Livgren starts his self-motivational speech right from the beginning:

"'Carry on my wayward son
There'll be peace when you are done
Lay your weary head to rest
Don't you cry no more'

"Throughout the song, Livgren talks about rising above his downtrodden state—and carrying on...

"Although Livgren became an evangelical Christian in 1980, he said the songs he wrote up until that point, including 'Carry On Wayward Son' [which peaked at #11 on *Billboard's* 100 in 1977] and the band's 1977 hit 'Dust in the Wind'—weren't religious but centered more about 'searching' for something.

"'I felt a profound urge to "Carry On" and continue the search,' said Livgren in a 1984 interview. 'I saw myself as a "Wayward Son," alienated from the ultimate reality, and yet striving to know it or him. The positive note at the end, *surely heaven waits for you*, seemed strange and premature, but I felt impelled to include it in the lyrics. It proved to be prophetic.'"[2]

Don't Fear the Reaper

CARRY ON WAYWARD SON

Songwriter: Kerry Livgren
Performed by Kansas
https://www.youtube.com/watch?v=yUkRDOIh_7I

Related Thoughts

In the article titled, "Kansas' wayward sons carrying on message," Eric Minton writes:

"Kerry Livgren, the man who writes most of Kansas' music and lyrics, is a born-again Christian, and has been expressing his religious convictions musically since his conversion at 3 a.m. July 25, 1979. Though he can pin down the exact moment of his conversion, Livgren, 32, said it was not a sudden revelation.

"'It was the culmination of a very long and diligent spiritual search,' he [Livgren] said in a phone interview from New Orleans last week.

"'It (Christianity) is the only culmination that is possible in a diligent and relentless spiritual search. Truth being an absolute, when one continues seeking, eventually he will arrive at the absolute. That came at 3 a.m.' Prior to his conversion, Livgren used his vast song and lyric writing abilities to play out for Kansas' audience his spiritual search through many different religions."[3]

"Born-again Christian" means Christ's divine presence is born within via the "Spirit of Christ,"[4] which is the Spirit of Truth.

During an interview, Livgren said:

"[O]ne night at 3:00 in the morning after a concert in Indianapolis IN, I was in a hotel room by myself. And I got this little Hal Lindsey book.... I was kind of skimming through it. He [Lindsey] had these little diagrams of what Jesus did on the Cross, and what it actually meant, and who he actually was. And it got to the part where Lindsey said something like, 'If he [Christ] was actually raised from the dead what does that mean? That means He's alive right now as you're reading this.' And that hit me like a train. And I guess what happened... I kind of surrendered, you know. I've been searching for God so long. I was weary. I didn't want to be a Christian, but I got on my knees and I surrendered. And I said if this is true then I don't care if I don't like it. I want the truth. And at that moment, I became somebody different; it totally changed me. It fulfilled everything I'd ever been looking for."[5]

When I first arrived at UConn (the main campus) in 1977, the radio airwaves were filled with "Carry On Wayward Son." I was one with that song. I was going to "carry on"—whatever that meant.

For me, that song was looking at me, as if God Himself was the narrator, speaking to me: "Surely heaven waits for you." Yet, like Kerry Livgren, I had no clue how we—as mere mortals—could know such a thing. Yet, Livgren said it proved to be prophetic: His lyrics were in fact a personal prophecy. Livgren's search brought him to divine truth. Christ said:

> "Truly, truly I say to you, whoever hears My word and believes in Him who sent Me has eternal life and shall not come into condemnation, but has passed from death into life."[6]

Eternal life means eternal life.

And in a search for divine truth, this is revealed to us:

> Christianity is the only major faith in the world where we arrive by the work of someone else, Christ. The kingdom of God is within us—upon our belief (of who Christ really is).

That's why Kerry Livgren could speak so confidently: It wasn't up to him to push his own soul—by his own works— into this eternal, spiritual kingdom.

Looking back to the Crucifixion, we see this spiritual reality: crossing the wall from death to (spiritual) life (Heaven awaits). On the Cross, Christ promised Paradise to a condemned criminal (crucified alongside Him). In that moment... Christ removed all condemnation and clothed him with divine righteousness. The criminal... *believed*.

> "Then he [the condemned criminal] said to Jesus, 'Lord, remember me when You come into Your kingdom.' Jesus said to him, 'Truly, I tell you, today you will be with Me in Paradise.'"[7]

1. https://www.loudersound.com/features/thestory-behind-carry-on-wayward-son-by-kansas. Retrieval date: July 12, 2023.
2. https://americansongwriter.com/the-storybehind-the-autobiographical-kansas-

hit-carry-onwayward-son/.
Retrieval date: August 21, 2023.
3. https://www.oklahoman.com/story/news/1982/07/22/kansas-wayward-sons-carrying-message/62878005007/.
Retrieval date: July 12, 2023.
4. **Romans 8:9.**
5. https://www.youtube.com/watch?v=JEzHz1aGyec.
Retrieval date: July 3, 2023.
6. **John 5:24.**
7. **Luke 23:42, 43.**

William Ayles, D.D.

6 Stairway to Heaven

"This is a song of hope."[1] —Robert Plant

"Robert Plant spent much of the '70s answering questions about the lyrics he wrote for 'Stairway.' When asked why the song was so popular, he said it could be its 'abstraction,' adding, 'Depending on what day it is, I still interpret the song a different way – and I wrote the lyrics.' The lyrics take some pretty wild turns, but the beginning of the song is about a woman who accumulates money, only to find out the hard way her life had no meaning and will not get her into heaven. This is the only part Plant would really explain, as he said it was 'a woman getting everything she wanted without giving anything back.'"[2]

William Ayles, D.D.

STAIRWAY TO HEAVEN

Songwriters: Jimmy Page / Robert Anthony Plant Performed by Led Zeppelin
https://www.youtube.com/watch?v=xbhCPt6PZIU

Related Thoughts

In the article titled, "What do Led Zeppelin's 'Stairway to Heaven' Lyrics Mean?" Jacob Uitti writes:

"The most crucial lyrics in the song are,

> 'Yes there are two paths you can go by, But in the long run, There's still time to change the road you're on, And it makes me wonder.'

"This idea of two paths is personified in the song by the woman, entitled, who thinks she can 'buy' a stairway to heaven, who thinks all that glitters is 'gold' and who believes, sings Plant, 'If the stores are all closed/With a word she can get what she came for.' However, there is another path.... This is what the singer hopes will happen to all people, especially the woman—a brush with reason, or logic."3

In the article titled, "The Meaning of Led Zeppelin's 'Stairway to Heaven,'" Chris Huber writes:

"Penned by Robert Plant, the lyrics to 'Stairway to Heaven' that begins as a critique on an overly materialistic society, suggesting that spending your entire life collecting material possessions is a fruitless endeavor, as it won't get you to heaven, and you can't use any of it when you get there, anyway.

"We can see that the woman Plant sings about is quite accustomed to having things done her way, as he suggests that after she buys her way into heaven, the stores there will open their doors for her well after closing time because she is just that special.

"However, this woman's life is telling her as blatantly as if there were a sign on the wall that her pursuit of riches and materialism will offer her nothing in the afterlife. She chooses to ignore this, because she wants to see for herself, as she has seen things to be not as they seem in the past.

"From there, the song shifts into a more spiritual perspective, and Plant shifts his own perspective into the first person. This coincides with additional layers being added to the song's arrangement, contributing to a gradual buildup that occurs through the first part of the song.

"In this way, 'Stairway to Heaven' can be seen as an allegory for one's journey through life, and the search for meaning and understanding through it all.

"As the song goes on, the lyrics become more abstract, as Plant continues to explore the calling of his spirit. He recalls a feeling of looking to the west with a strong desire to leave, or to run away from his problems and worries.

"Then we have the metaphor of smoke rising through the trees, which has been taken to mean many things by many different people. But the gist is that it is an eerily threatening thing to see, such as an approaching army, while people outside the forest stand and watch in anticipation of the threat to come.

"However, all of this is happening in Plant's thoughts, again suggesting the meaning to be metaphorical of one's journey through life and the challenges you may face along the way.

"In the next segment, Plant offers some more hopeful imagery: *'And a new day will dawn for those who stand long, and the forests will echo with laughter.'*

"Here we can see the people whispering among themselves of a hope for salvation 'if we all call the tune.' This can be seen as an ode to the power of music, suggesting that it is capable of fighting off the powerful forces of darkness.

"This tune brings a new beginning for those who were able to face the darkness, with the smoke in the forests replaced by the sounds of laughter coming from within. From the spiritual perspective, this can be taken to mean that Plant has found a peaceful balance within his life once again, and he can once again find pleasure in the simple joys.

"While the line about having a bustle in your hedgerow may sound sexual, Robert Plant himself has explained that the lyric is really about the new beginning that comes with the dawn of spring. This is suggested with the next line, that sings of 'a spring clean for the May queen.'

"From here we can derive the meaning that when things get shaken up in life it can be alarming, but oftentimes those shakeups lead us to new opportunities and levels of understanding that we couldn't have had before.

"To continue the hopeful message, Plant sings of the age-old metaphor for taking different paths in life. His lyrics suggest that no matter how far you've gone down the wrong path, there is always time to make a change for the better.

"In the next verse, ... Plant sings again about the call of the spirit, and suggests that the meaning of life can be found within the journey itself.

"Plant also brings back the piper from earlier in the song, who calls for participation in his song of freedom. This begins with humming the song in one's head, and then hearing it in the wind.

"He addresses the woman from the first part of the song again, too, and tells her that the stairway to heaven she seeks can be found within the song of the wind. This means that in order to find salvation within life itself, one must follow the calling that comes from within their own heart.

"Finally, we reach the climax of the song — a full minute of instrumental breakdown that releases the tension that had been building during the previous six minutes of [the] song.

"Then, we have the final lyrics, representing the final revelations that one might have near the end of their life, with 'shadows taller than our soul.'"[4]

IN MY TIME OF DYING

In the 2015 article titled, "The Gospel According to Led Zeppelin," Steve Sanchez writes:

"[Robert] Plant sang the Gospel truth in one of my favorites called 'In My Time of Dying.' ... Perhaps Robert read his Bible? He is, of course, echoing [the apostle] Paul's words: 'we who are still alive and remain on the earth will be caught up [raptured] in the clouds to meet the Lord in the air. Then we will be with the Lord forever' (1 Thessalonians 4:17)."5

https://www.youtube.com/watch?v=fGUEAFjcPYM

SATAN, YOUR KINGDOM MUST COME DOWN

In 2010, Robert Plant released the album, Band of Joy—with his backing group: Band of Joy.

The release included the song, "Satan, Your Kingdom Must Come Down." Robert nailed it.

https://www.youtube.com/watch?v=Ais53rladFU

In the 2011 article titled, "Robert Plant: the showman must go on," Ed Vulliamy quoted Robert:

"I'm just incredibly fortunate that my eyes and ears have been opened. I have to be honest with myself and remove as much of the repetition and fakery as is humanly possible.

"If you're a singer, you can never say this is where the voyage ends, the job is never done. Once you have got it, you cannot sit on it. I have to try and change the landscape, whatever it is. I have to find a new place to ply my trade, to get lost in another place, and locate myself again. I'm an older man now and so it's even more important."[6]

In a 1994 interview, Jimmy Page wore a t-shirt, "Recovering Catholic."[7] I too was raised Roman Catholic. As a Roman Catholic, I did gain a sense of awe for Christ. However, I never understood the meaning of the words that (ultimately) set me free: "Christ in you, the hope of glory."[8] (See the Epilogue.) Later in life, Jimmy Page reflected on his own spiritual journey—and he summed it up: "love of all things mystical and magical, all things bright and beautiful."[9]

"Stairway to Heaven"

Jimmy Page (guitarist) composed the music. Robert Plant (vocalist) wrote the lyrics—and he got it right. There is a stairway to Heaven. And it cannot be bought. In the song, Plant connects the "stairway" to the "wind." In the Gospels, Christ connects the "Spirit" to the "wind":

"The wind blows wherever it pleases. You hear its sound, but you cannot tell where it comes from or where it is going. So it is with everyone born of the Spirit [of Truth]."[10]

All those years ago, in my search for truth, I realized this: The Spirit of Truth is the key to the door that leads to the stairway to Heaven (a.k.a. immortality). This Spirit is a gift, and thus, access to the stairway to Heaven is a gift.

In contrast, the woman in the song is buying a stairway to Heaven. Futile. Her vanity distorted her perception of reality. She bent her knees to a false god: gold.

Consider the words of Christ on this: "What good is it for someone to gain the whole world, yet forfeit their soul?"[11]

1. https://www.rollingstone.com/music/musicfeatures/robert-plant-alison-krauss-led-zeppelin1396022/. Retrieval: June 23, 2023.
2. https://www.songfacts.com/facts/ledzeppelin/stairway-to-heaven. Retrieval date: June 23, 2023.
3. https://americansongwriter.com/what-do-ledzeppelins-stairway-to-heaven-lyrics-mean/. Retrieval date: June 30, 2023.
4. https://extrachill.com/led-zeppelin-stairway-toheaven-meaning. Retrieval date: August 19, 2023.
5. https://stonethepreacher.com/the-gospelaccording-to-led-zeppelin/. Retrieval date: May 27, 2024.
6. https://www.theguardian.com/music/2011/jan/30/robert-plant-band-joy-interview. Retrieval date: May 29, 2024.
7. https://www.youtube.com/watch?v=0mxnvpis7Xc &t=1s. Retrieval: August 19, 2023.
8. Colossians 1:27.
9. https://www.youtube.com/watch?v=7uEesEj1G-g. Retrieval date: May 28, 2023.
10. John 3:8.
11. Mark 8:36.

ACT TWO

William Ayles, D.D.

7 Jesus is Just Alright

In the article titled, "The 1966 version of 'Jesus is Just Alright' will knock your socks off," J-P Mauro writes:

"'Jesus Is Just Alright,' written by Arthur Reid Reynolds... was first recorded by Reynolds' own group, The Art Reynolds Singers, for their 1966 album, Tellin' It Like It Is.

"In the 1970s, there was a run on the market for pop music with spiritual connections. Songs like 'Spirit in the Sky' by Norman Greenbaum and 'Morning Has Broken' by Cat Stevens were dominating the airwaves when The Doobie Brothers dropped their second studio album, Toulouse Street, and made 'Jesus Is Just Alright' a top 50 hit.

"But not many people knew that it was actually a cover... of a cover.

"The Doobie Brothers were introduced to the tune from The Byrds' 1969 album, Ballad of Easy Rider. This is why The Doobie Brothers' version is much closer in its arrangement to The Byrds' version, rather than Reynolds' original. In order to fit with the 1970s style, The

William Ayles, D.D.

Doobie Brothers added a bridge and extra refrains, which elongated the tune."[1]

Jesus is Just Alright

Songwriter: Arthur Reid Reynolds
Performed by The Doobie Brothers
https://www.youtube.com/watch?v=bQ2T107k1FU

Related Thoughts

In the article titled, "Monday Morning Music, 'Jesus is Just Alright,'" Alex Doroit writes:

"Written and performed by The Art Reynolds Singers in 1966, 'Jesus Is Just Alright' was meant to be a response to the 'Hippie' culture of the time. The word 'alright' of course being a popular slang term of the decade.

"The Doobie Brothers liked the song enough to record their own version. It became one of the biggest hits of their career. 40 years later, the song is still a staple on classic rock radio.

"Now, who's to say if anyone in The Doobie Brothers is a Christian. None of the band members are publicly religious. But something about this gospel song spoke to them.

"In much the same way, it's hard to tell if the song has made a significant impact on the faith of people who listen to it. After all, it's kind of an ambiguous tune. It doesn't really proselytize. It doesn't condemn. It just says Jesus seems like a cool guy.

"Still, for over 40 years the term 'Jesus Is Just Alright' has been ingrained in pop culture. The phrase has been sung over movie trailers, in rock halls, in people's cars driving to work. It's been sandwiched in between countless other contemporary songs on the radio for decades.

"The song has inarguably brought Jesus to the forefront of popular culture. Whether intentionally or not The Doobie Brothers continue to bring His name to millions of listeners' minds for 3 minutes at a time when they wouldn't normally be thinking of Him.

"Art Reynolds could not have had a clue when he was writing 'Jesus Is Just Alright' the impact it would have on the world. He was just doing his job. He had no idea who was watching and listening to his work. He had no idea the way his work would spread across the world."[2]

As presented in "Songfacts":

"['Jesus is Just Alright'] is a very spiritual song with a pretty clear message about loving Jesus. Very few mainstream hits are so unambiguously in praise of Jesus, and was a very odd message coming from The Doobie Brothers. [Tom] Johnston told Songfacts: 'The funny thing about that, we weren't anti-religious. We weren't anything. We were just musicians out playing a gig.'"[3]

I went to a Doobie Brothers concert along with high school buddies of mine. We had excellent seats, close to the stage. We literally looked up to the band; we felt the intensity of the music—which increased the impact of the performance. The Doobies put on a powerful show. My thanks to the band. Jesus is just alright with me. His words are alright—and frankly, unprecedented. His words ask us to reflect on what really matters. He said:

> "Blessed are those who hunger and thirst for righteousness, for they shall be filled. Blessed are the merciful, for they shall obtain mercy. Blessed are the pure in heart, for they shall see God. Blessed are the peacemakers, for they shall be called the sons of God."[4]

1. https://aleteia.org/2018/05/07/the-1966-versionof-jesus-is-just-alright-will-knock-your-socks-off/. Retrieval date: August 22, 2023.
2. https://popgodblog.com/2014/10/06/mondaymorning-music-jesus-is-just-alright/. Retrieval date: July 12, 2023.
3. https://www.songfacts.com/facts/the-doobiebrothers/jesus-is-just-alright. Retrieval date: July 12, 2023.
4. Matthew 5:6–9.

William Ayles, D.D.

8 All the Way

In the article titled, "Top 10 Rockers Who Found God," Andy Greene writes:

"Grand Funk Railroad were one of the most successful rock bands of the 1970s, but when they stopped selling albums and tickets in the early 1980s frontman Mark Farner turned to Jesus and turned his life around. He angered some fans by re-recording Grand Funk's classic 'Some Kind of Wonderful' with new spiritual lyrics in 1991, but they forgave him later in the decade when he reunited with the rest of Grand Funk for a triumphant tour. Today, the group tours without him, but he plays regularly as a solo act — performing a mix of Grand Funk classics and Christian rock tunes."[1]

In the article titled, "The Testimony of Mark Farner," Farner states:

"Since all scripture is inspired by God, I believe that it is the only source of true instruction and righteousness, and therefore the only authority by which those of us who long for truth and holiness can look for council."[2]

All the Way

Songwriter: Mark Farner
Performed by Mark Farner
https://www.youtube.com/watch?v=sVoV7kwFccw

Related Thoughts

In the article titled, "Mark Farner: Guitarist talks Funk and Forgiveness," Mark Voger writes:

"Farner — who sang and played on such Grand Funk hits as 'I'm Your Captain,' 'Some Kind of Wonderful' and 'The Loco-motion' — ... says his special brand of faith keeps him going in dark times. 'I'm Christian, but I'm a different kind of Christian, especially since I had my pacemaker put in,' says the Michigan native, 65. 'I died and came back twice, so I know what it's like to be outside of this body, and to be in the arms and the presence of love.'"[3]

In the September 2023 edition of *Tru Rock Revival*, Abbe Davis writes:

"Mark has performed Christian Rock and the hit songs from Grand Funk, as well as many of his hit songs in shows he still does with his American Band. Most every 4th of July holiday you will hear that song, 'Red, White & Blue,' as the fireworks light up the sky. That song is the genuine message of hope and faith that exemplifies Mark Farner. It is an anthem for our country."[4]

In the 2016 article titled, "Concert Preview: Mark Farner Bringing the Grand Funk to Ridgefield," John Voket—of *The Newtown Bee* [Newtown, Connecticut publication]—writes:

William Ayles, D.D.

"In an interview with The Newtown Bee ahead of his January 20 [2016] tour stop at The Ridgefield Playhouse [Connecticut], Farner was not shy about discussing his near death experiences, as well as the immense pride and spiritual connectedness he derives from his Native American heritage.

"Farner said that heritage is further and interestingly mixed, because his great grandmother married a Jewish groom, and more recently, Farner himself became a born-again Christian after his pair of near death experiences.

"The classic rocker also talked a lot about music, his touring band, and jolt he gets mixing brand new music with classic rock favorites that still get audiences on their feet, dancing in the aisles, and singing along to Farner's kit bag of familiar tunes he penned for Grand Funk between the late '60s through mid-'70s.

"As their lead vocalist, lead guitarist and principal songwriter the group rocketed to rock stardom following a show-stealing performance before 180,000 people at the Atlanta International Pop Festival in 1969, according to Farner's web bio.

"After enjoying moderate success touring and generating several lukewarm regional hits, Grand Funk's third album, Closer To Home, was one of the group's most successful and included the classic Farner anthem 'I'm Your Captain' (a/k/a 'Closer To Home') as well as 'Aimless Lady,' 'Mean Mistreater' and 'Sin's A Good Man's Brother,' all written by Farner.

"Due in no small part to his strong and steady vocals, mastery of guitar and stage charisma, Grand Funk was one of those very few bands who really was better live than in the studio, according to biographer Kristofer Engelhardt. So it was no surprise when their album Grand Funk Live reached the Top Five.

"However, all of this paled in comparison to the group's sold out performance at New York's 55,000seat Shea Stadium in 1971. Not since The Beatles had any group sold out Shea, and GFR still holds the record.

"Speaking of the Beatles, in 1995, Mark accepted an invitation to join Ringo Starr's All-Starr Band where his show-stealing performances proved audiences were still hungry for Mark and Grand Funk's music.

"Looking toward the future with great enthusiasm, Farner told The Bee he is hoping [his] new album project will take off with new record company support, and said he was pleased to be able to hand over the reins after putting out several previous releases on his own.

William Ayles, D.D.

"While that new project will feature mostly new material, Farner said he has re-worked one of his biggest '70s hits for his 21st Century fans.

"'We've re-cut "Some Kind of Wonderful" which will be on the new release,' Farner said.

"Settling down Farner on the line from his current home in snowy northern Michigan, we opened the conversation talking about his Native American bloodlines.

"Newtown Bee: 'So I understand besides all the success you've enjoyed as a rock star, you've also been recognized as result of your family's Native American heritage.'

"Mark Farner: 'My mother's grandmother was fullblood Cherokee, and I was given a medal of honor by the Cherokee Nation, as well as a prayer quilt by the Lakota-Sioux Nation. It was a great honor. Even though I'm not in the Rock & Roll Hall of Fame, it means more to me because this is my heart — it's who I am. And it honors my mother and grandmother, too.'

"Bee: 'And more recently you've had some success on the Contemporary Christian front.'

"Farner: 'It mixes just fine. A few years ago when I had my pacemaker put in I exited the bone suit and went to heaven — in fact it happened twice. I heard the doctor telling my wife, "we've got him back twice but there's no guarantee we'll get him back a third time, so we have to get him to the operating room stat." Then it turned into MASH 4077 with people running around. I'll tell you, being temporarily put back where I started from was like being safer than in my mother's womb — I knew all things in that state of mind, and you relate to all things, no mystery. So on the way back, I'm hearing this doctor talking to my wife, I'm thinking [expletive], it was so good over there. But I still have a lot of responsibility back here. But I was shown things over there that I could turn into human words. That's why I'm free in Christ, and that's my choice.'"[5]

In 1991, Mark Farner released his album, Some Kind of Wonderful—which included the song, "All the Way."[6] In the song, He repeats an emphatic declaration: to "surrender." What exactly is Mark Farner surrendering to? Christ. Divine truth. When Christ taught in the Holy Land, He was the living, breathing Word of God—in the flesh:

> "The Word [of God] became flesh and dwelt among us, and we saw His glory, the glory as the only Son of the Father, full of grace and truth."[7]

1. https://www.rollingstone.com/music/musiclists/top-10-rockers-who-found-god-20985/markfarner-240873/. Retrieval date: June 23, 2023.

2. http://grandfunkrock.com/farnerfiler/testimon.htm. Retrieval date: February 21, 2024.
3. https://www.nj.com/entertainment/2014/05/mark_farner_grand_funk.html. Retrieval date: August 21, 2023.
4. https://www.trurockrevival.com/mark-farnerformerly-of-grand-funk. Retrieval date: August 21, 2023.
5. http://www.newtownbee.com/01152016/concertpreview-mark-farner-bringing-the-grand-funk-toridgefield/. Retrieval date: September 6, 2023.
6. https://markfarner.com/music-2/. Retrieval date: September 6, 2023.
7. John 1:14.

9 Saved

"**I** knew Jimi Hendrix. I knew Janis Joplin. If they knew then what I know now, they'd still be here."[1] — Bob Dylan

In the article titled, "Top 10 Rockers Who Found God," Andy Greene writes:

"No major rock star has ever undergone as radical a religious transformation as Bob Dylan. The man who once wrote 'Don't follow leaders, Watch your parking meters' launched a tour in 1979 behind his gospel LP Slow Train Coming in which he didn't play any of his old songs. Between tunes he preached fire and brimstone. 'I told you "The Times They Are AChangin'" and they did!' he preached to the crowd one night in 1979. 'I told you the answer was "Blowin' In The Wind" and it was! And I'm saying to you now, Jesus is coming back and he is! There is no other way to salvation... Jesus is coming back to set up his kingdom in Jerusalem for a thousand years.'"[2]

SAVED

Songwriters: Bob Dylan / Tim Drummond
Performed by Bob Dylan
https://www.youtube.com/watch?v=MIUNftAi_z4

Related Thoughts

In the 1980 *Los Angeles Times* article titled, "Bob Dylan's Song of Salvation," Robert Hilburn writes:

"Bob Dylan has finally confirmed in an interview what he has been saying in his music for 18 months: He is a born-again Christian.

"Dylan, 39, said that he accepted Jesus in his heart in 1978 after a 'vision and feeling' during which the room moved: 'There was a presence in the room that couldn't have been anybody but Jesus.'

"He was initially reluctant to tell his friends or put his feeling into songs, but he was so committed to his gospel music by late 1979 that he did not perform any of his songs during a tour. He said that he feared the old material might be 'anti-God.'

"Believing now that the old and new songs are compatible, Dylan again sings such stinging rockers as 'Like a Rolling Stone' alongside such born-again treatises as 'Gotta Serve Somebody.'

"Sitting in his Los Angeles hotel room before a concert, Dylan, whose family is Jewish, sat on a couch and smoked a cigarette as he discussed his religious experience.

"'The funny thing is a lot of people think that Jesus comes into a person's life only when they are either down and out or are miserable or just old and withering away,' Dylan said. 'That's not the way it was for me. I was doing fine. I had come a long way in just the year we were on the road [1978]. I was relatively content, but a very close friend of mine mentioned a couple of things to me and one of them was Jesus.'

"'Well, the whole idea of Jesus was foreign to me. I said to myself, "I can't deal with that. Maybe later." But later it occurred to me that I trusted this person and I had nothing to do with the next couple of days so I called the person back and said I was willing to listen about Jesus.'

"Through a friend, Dylan met two young pastors.

"'I was kind of skeptical, but I was also open,' he said. 'I certainly wasn't cynical. I asked lots of questions, questions like, "What's the son of God, what's all that mean?" and, "What does it mean – dying for my sins?"'

"Slowly, Dylan began to accept that 'Jesus was real and I wanted that… I knew that He wasn't going to come into my life and make it miserable, so one thing led to another… until I had this feeling, this vision and feeling.'

"Dylan, the most acclaimed songwriter of the rock era, had been unwilling to grant interviews since the release last year of the gospel-dominated 'Slow Train Coming' album, suggesting that anyone who wanted to know what he felt could simply listen to that work.

"The album was a passionate testimony to Christian salvation, devotion and doctrine.

Though the album became one of Dylan's biggest sellers, many of his fans felt confused, even betrayed: The man who once urged his audience to question all authority was suddenly embracing what some believed was the most simplistic of religious sentiments.

"Even when he returned last spring with another gospel album, the less commercially successful 'Saved,' rumors abounded that he had abandoned the born-again beliefs. But Dylan's shows on his present tour have refuted that speculation. Ten of his 17 songs on opening night were from the last two albums.

"In the interview…, Dylan stressed that his beliefs are deeply rooted: 'It's in my system.'

"'I truly had a born-again experience, if you want to call it that. It's an overused term, but it's something that people can relate to. It happened in 1978.'

"'I always knew there was a God or a creator of the universe and a creator of the mountains and the sea and all that kind of thing, but I wasn't conscious of Jesus and what that had to do with the Supreme Creator.'

"'Most of the people I know don't believe that Jesus was resurrected, that He is alive. It's like He was just another prophet or something, one of many good people. That's not the way it was any longer for me. I had always read the Bible, but I only looked at it as literature. I was never really instructed in it in a way that was meaningful to me.'"3

During one of his Gospel Tours, Dylan said:

"I read the Bible a lot, it just happens I do…. And I've been reading all kinds of books my whole life and I really never found any truth in any of them. These things in the Bible, they seem to uplift me and tell me the truth."4

Regarding the truth, there is a fascinating exchange in the Bible between Christ and Pontus Pilate (the Roman governor of Judea):

> "Pilate said to Him, 'Then are You a king?' Jesus answered, 'You say correctly that I am a king. For this reason I was born, and for this reason I came into the world, to bear witness to the truth. Everyone who is of the truth hears My voice.' Pilate said to Him, 'What is truth?'"5

Pilate asked a good question: "What is truth?" In 2000 years, what's changed?

The same question still pulses in the airwaves of life.

How do we respond to it?

Either Jesus told the truth about the truth, or He didn't.

Jesus is also referred to as "'Immanuel,' which is interpreted, 'God with us.'"[6]

"Immanuel."

If there ever was divine truth on this planet, it would be Immanuel. And we would expect this truth to be backed up by a divine presence. And it is. Christ said:

> "[W]hen He, the Spirit of Truth (the Truth giving Spirit) comes, He will guide you into all the Truth (the whole, full Truth)."[7]

This Spirit is spiritual truth; it is another dimension of life; it is a source of transformation and inspiration. How else could someone like Bob Dylan flip a switch, produce 3 gospel albums, and exhibit such passion?

In the article titled, "Top 10 Rockers Who Found God," Andy Greene writes:

"By the mid-1980s the singer [Bob Dylan] born Robert Allen Zimmerman had returned to his

Jewish roots, no doubt making his mother a very happy woman."8

From a spiritual perspective, the Spirit of Truth remains (born) within. As Christ Himself said, the Spirit will be us forever:

> "I will pray the Father, and He will give you another Counselor [Comforter], that He may be with you forever: the Spirit of truth, whom the world cannot receive, for it does not see Him, neither does it know Him. But you know Him, for He lives with you, and will be in you."9

SOLID ROCK

Another song on Dylan's album, Saved, is "Solid Rock." It is a Dylan classic.

https://www.youtube.com/watch?v=CIJQ-7n9Vbc

Don't Fear the Reaper

A SATISFIED MIND

The lyrics of "A Satisfied Mind" say it all.

https://www.youtube.com/watch?v=lTfPEu8YlBI

1. AARP The Magazine, (February/March, 2015), p 27.
2. https://www.rollingstone.com/music/musiclists/top-10-rockers-who-found-god-20985/bobdylan-52-241017/. Retrieval date: July 4, 2023.
3. https://www.washingtonpost.com/archive/lifesty le/1980/11/24/bob-dylans-song-ofsalvation/1fba5ce3-e6fa-40dc-8a17a384bb537643/. Retrieval date: August 23, 2023. 4. Inside Bob Dylan's Jesus Years: Busy Being Born Again! (2008). Tubi. Retrieval date: September 29, 2023.
5. John 18:37, 38.
6. Matthew 1:23.

7. John 16:13, *Amplified, Classic Edition*.
8. https://www.rollingstone.com/music/musiclists/top-10-rockers-who-found-god-20985/bobdylan-52-241017/. Retrieval date: September 9, 2023.
9. John 14:16, 17.

10   Personal Jesus

In the 2022 article titled, "'More than an iconic rebel': New Johnny Cash documentary focuses on his Christian faith," Marcus K. Dowling writes:

"The key to understanding Johnny Cash is through his born-again Christianity, according to a documentary released this week."[1]

As found in the article titled, "Johnny Cash's Beautiful Cover of 'Personal Jesus'":

"'Personal Jesus' was originally a song performed by <u>Depeche Mode</u>. The electric band is originally from the UK. The song was the first one to make it to the US Top 40 since 1984's

William Ayles, D.D.

'People Are People,' and was their first gold-certified single in the US.

"When the singer [Johnny Cash] was asked why he did a cover of this song, he has this to say: 'I heard that as a gospel song. And if you think of it as a gospel song, it works really well. We didn't have any major disagreement over that song, I just heard that a couple of people had recorded it, the writer wanted me to try it, and I did, and I loved it. And I went for it.'

"The song is more stripped down because Johnny Cash wanted it to be more personal. He knows the message of the song so he wants to give justice to his cover. This is why Johnny is respected not only by the country fans but all music fans. It's because of the passion that he pours in his performances."[2]

Personal Jesus: Johnny Cash

Songwriter: Martin Gore
Performed by Johnny Cash
https://www.youtube.com/watch?v=lw3UonQwNco

Related Thoughts

Personal Jesus: Depeche Mode

In the 2022 article titled, "The Depeche Mode song inspired by Elvis Presley," Tyler Golsen writes:

"When it came to the track's inspiration, [Martin] Gore [of Depeche Mode] cited one of Cash's contemporaries, Elvis Presley, as the launching point for the song's lyrics.

"Specifically, it was Priscilla Presley's 1985 biography Elvis and Me that caused Gore to contemplate ownership and control in a relationship. 'It's a song about being a Jesus for somebody else, someone to give you hope and care,' Gore told SPIN in 1990. 'It's about how Elvis Presley was her man and her mentor and how often that happens in love relationships; how everybody's heart is like a god in some way, and that's not a very balanced view of someone, is it?'"[3]

William Ayles, D.D.

https://www.youtube.com/watch?v=W6hcDAuJIiQ

"Speaking to Entertainment Weekly in 2017, Depeche Mode frontman Dave Gahan reflected on Johnny Cash covering their track…. '[I]t's a great version, just fantastic. But it really propelled the song to another dimension.'"4

As found in the article titled, "Johnny Cash Quotes":

"As one of the most popular musicians of all time, Johnny Cash influenced many with his country rock/gospel sound. Although throughout his early career, 'The Man in Black' became addicted to drugs and alcohol, he later cleaned his life up and reaffirmed his Christian faith.

"In honor of Johnny Cash's birthday on February 26, here are… Johnny Cash quotes on God and faith:

"'There was nothing left of me. I had drifted so far away from God and every stabilizing force in my life that I felt there was no hope... My separation from Him, the deepest and most ravaging of the various kinds of loneliness I'd felt over the years, seemed finally complete. It wasn't. I thought I'd left Him, but He hadn't left me. I felt something very powerful start to happen to me, a sensation of utter peace, clarity, and sobriety. Then my mind started focusing on God.' "'How well I have learned that there is no fence to sit on between heaven and hell. There is a deep, wide gulf, a chasm, and in that chasm is no place for any man.'

"'Creative people have to be fed from the divine source. I have to get fed. I had to get filled up in order to pour out.'

"'When God forgave me, I figured I'd better do it too.'

"'The Master of Life's been good to me. He has given me strength to face past illnesses, and victory in the face of defeat. He has given me life and joy where others saw oblivion. He Has given new purpose to live for, new services to render and old wounds to heal. Life and love go on, let the music play.'"[5]

Johnny Cash is right: We have a personal Jesus. Jesus said:

William Ayles, D.D.

"I stand at the door and knock. If anyone hears My voice and opens the door, I will come in and dine [commune] with him, and he with Me."[6]

Man in Black

Cash's song, "Man in Black," sums up his life—and the meaning he found.

https://www.youtube.com/watch?v=0Dd32K-mOVw

Johnny Cash is a LEGEND. And he is a voice for Christ.

'Nuff said.

1. https://www.tennessean.com/story/entertainment/2022/12/08/new-johnny-cash-documentary-focuses-on-hischristian-faith/69689932007/. Retrieval date: July 12, 2023.

2. https://www.countrythangdaily.com/johnnycash-cover-personal-jesus/. Retrieval date: July 12, 2023.
3. https://faroutmagazine.co.uk/the-depeche-modesong-inspired-by-elvis-presley/. Retrieval date: May 30, 2024.
4. https://faroutmagazine.co.uk/depeche-modereact-johnny-cash-personal-jesus/. Retrieval date: July 13, 2023.
5. https://www.beliefnet.com/entertainment/music/ 2009/05/johnny-cash-quotes.aspx. Retrieval date: July 12, 2023.
6. Revelation 3:20.

William Ayles, D.D.

11   Spirit in the Sky

In the *Rolling Stone* article titled, "Norman Greenbaum on 'Spirit in the Sky' at 50: 'The Interest in It Just Doesn't Wane,'" Angie Martoccio writes:

"Fifty years after 'Spirit in the Sky' became a hit, singer-songwriter Norman Greenbaum looks back on his immortal fuzz-rock anthem.

"Greenbaum spoke with *RS* [*Rolling Stone*] about how a Jew managed to write a song about Jesus... 'Well, I've never written a religious song.... I just sat down, and it all came together.'

"'At first the record company said, "Gee, they don't play anything like this on Top 20,"' the singer songwriter [Greenbaum] tells *Rolling Stone* of his immortal boogie-rock anthem. 'But obviously they were wrong. We always knew it was going to be a hit. It just sounded too good.'

"The song came out in the U.S. in January 1970. Propelled by a chugging, bluesy riff and featuring lyrics about befriending Jesus and preparing for death, it peaked at Number

Three on *Billboard's* Hot 100 and was certified gold.

"In the 50 years since its release, 'Spirit in the Sky' has never really gone away. The song has appeared in more than 30 commercials and 60 films.... 'I've got an audience that's coming around again,' Greenbaum, now 77, says over the phone from his home in California. 'The song started with kids' grandparents and then their parents and then they hear it in all these movies. Now there's a whole young generation that is into the song.'"[1]

SPIRIT IN THE SKY

Don't Fear the Reaper

Songwriter and Performed by Norman Greenbaum
https://www.youtube.com/watch?v=vRF072wuU6w

Related Thoughts

When "Spirit in the Sky" hit the radio, I bought the 45 single. Every summer, my cousin Glenn and his family visited us here in Connecticut, driving in from Illinois. During his visit in the summer of 1970, I played that song and listened to it with him, repeatedly. Glenn lamented there weren't more songs on the radio like "Spirit in the Sky."

That song was the first song I ever heard about Jesus Christ that was "cool." It was a catchy tune. And, most importantly, the singer sang confidently about the certainty of his destiny. Yes, that was and is... cool. Certainty is a wonderful thing.

William Ayles, D.D.

And Christ (our Good Shepherd) handed us the love of our Creator and the certainty of our future. Christ said of us:

> "My sheep hear My voice, and I know them, and they follow Me. I give them eternal life. They shall never perish, nor shall anyone snatch them from My hand. My Father, who has given them to Me, is greater than all. No one is able to snatch them from My Father's hand."[2]

My sister stumbled upon a YouTube video—which is perfectly suited for the young at heart: the Peanuts Gang singing "Spirit in the Sky."

https://www.youtube.com/watch?v=jGZ7t4v0RNc

1. https://www.rollingstone.com/music/musicfeatures/norman-greenbaum-interview-spirit-inthe-sky-934508/. Retrieval date: June 20, 2023.
2. John 10:27–29.

Shakespeare's Romeo & Juliet, some have speculated that the track was in some way promoting suicide. He [Dharma] spoke of this with the College Music Journal (CMJ) in 1995:

"'I felt that I had just achieved some kind of resonance with the psychology of people when I came up with that, I was actually kind of appalled when I first realized that some people were seeing it as an advertisement for suicide or something that was not my intention at all. It is, like, not to be afraid of it (as opposed to actively bring it about). It's basically a love song where the love transcends the actual physical existence of the partners.'

"In the introductory lyrics, Dharma sings about the end of life, saying that the two lovers times have come and gone. They were once here, but now they are passed and gone.

"Buck's lyrics assert that the seasons are not afraid of death, and neither is the wind, the sun, or the rain. Addressing a lover, Buck sings that they can be like the seasons, the wind, the sun, and the rain, and also not fear death. He encourages his lover to take his hand, be with him, and fly onward without fear of the reaper.

"Then, he suggests that 40,000 people die every single day, and that there is nothing to be done about it because there will be another 40,000 who die tomorrow. The key here is the lyric 'redefine happiness', as he is proposing that lovers find a way to be happy despite the inevitability of death."3

(Don't Fear) The Reaper

Songwriter: Donald Roeser (a.k.a. Buck Dharma) Performed by Blue Öyster Cult
https://www.youtube.com/watch?v=1yotUsdqyDg

Related Thoughts

By the time I turned 21 years old, the fear of death stuck to me like gum on my shoe. But soon thereafter, I found that candle in that cave. My fear of death ended; the eternal Spirit of Truth (that filled me) replaced that fear.

This truth—freed from that fear—is reflected in "(Don't Fear) The Reaper." Love does transcend death. Why should we wait in fear on the edge of eternal night when we can escape it?

Listen to how Christ broke Satan's power over us, and freed us from mortality and the fear of death:

> "[B]y his [Christ's] death he might break the power of him who holds the power of death— that is, the devil—and free those who all their lives were held in slavery by their fear of death."4

And Christ said:

> "I have not spoken on My own authority, but the Father who sent Me gave Me a command, what I should say and what I should speak. I know that His command is eternal life. Therefore what I say, I say as the Father tells me."5

1. https://www.guitarplayer.com/players/how-buckdharma-wrote-blue-oyster-cults-dont-fear-thereaper. Retrieval date: July 11, 2023.
2. https://americansongwriter.com/the-mortalmeaning-behind-blue-oyster-cults-1976-classicdont-fear-the-reaper/. Retrieval date: July 17, 2023.
3. https://extrachill.com/blue-oyster-cult-dont-fearthe-reaper-meaning. Retrieval date: August 20, 2023.
4. Hebrews 2:14, 15.
5. John 12:49, 50.

William Ayles, D.D.

THE ENCORE

William Ayles, D.D.

13   The Wall

"**E**very great composer I've ever looked up to has always refused to let the ways of the world dictate what their art would be."[1] —Kerry Livgren

"The Wall" appears on the 1976 Kansas' *Leftoverture* album. For me, the lyrics of "The Wall" paint a vivid picture: I'm in the picture.

I used to play this song in my headphones at UConn over and over, but I never really understood the depth of the lyrics... nor did I realize I was on one side of that wall—the material side.

William Ayles, D.D.

The beginning of the song places me squarely where I was at that time.

The end of the song places me squarely where I am now.

THE WALL

Songwriters: Kerry Livgren / Steve Walsh
Performed by Kansas
https://www.youtube.com/watch?v=bRJ5U49sJbI

Related Thoughts

Ironically, religious leaders can create their own walls between us and spirituality. Going back to 1980, I saw for the first time how religious walls are created: by replacing truth with dogma. I was stunned to see what Christ faced. Listen to how Christ laced into the religious hypocrites of His day:

> "[W]hy do you break the command of God for the sake of your tradition?"[2]

> "Woe to you, scribes and Pharisees [temple authorities], hypocrites! You shut the kingdom of heaven against men. For you neither enter yourselves, nor allow those who are entering to go in. Woe unto you, blind guides.... You serpents! You generation of vipers! How can you escape the judgment of hell?"[3]

Christ called out the "blind guides." And He revealed a tragic reality: An institution can take away the keys of eternal truth.

The religious machine of the temple churned out dogma. And that is exactly what Jesus said:

> "These people draw near to Me with their mouth, and honor Me with their lips, but their heart is far from Me. In vain they do worship Me, teaching as doctrines the precepts [rules] of men [religious dogma]."[4]

Rules of religious hypocrites.

Useless.

For Heaven's sake: We cannot afford to slumber in dogma on the wrong side of the wall.

Looking back to the time of Christ, we see the wall of darkness created by the religious authorities: they mocked Jesus—and conspired to kill Him. By hanging Jesus on a Cross, the deceived authorities thought they blotted out His spiritual light. Instead, the religious leaders played right into God's plan: God's Son became the ultimate sacrifice; a sinless man (Jesus) took (upon Himself) all our sins. And when we embrace Him for who He really is, He becomes our personal Jesus: Our sins go upon Him, and His righteousness goes upon us.

Christ's blood is the ransom to free us from our mortality: It is immortality through spirituality through Christ. Christ said:

> "[T]he Son of Man came not to be served, but to serve, and to give His life as a ransom for many."[5]

1. https://www.angelicwarlord.com/articles/kansas.h tml. Retrieval date: September 12, 2023.
2. Matthew 15:3.
3. Matthew 23:13, 16, 33.
4. Matthew 15:8, 9.
5. Mark 10:45.

14 Freedom

In the 2021 article titled, "Justin Bieber Makes First Appearance on Top Christian Albums Chart as 'Freedom' Debuts at No. 3," Jim Asker writes:

"Pop superstar Justin Bieber surprised his fans by releasing his first spiritual set, the six-song Freedom..., on Easter Sunday (April 4). [And it entered] Billboard's Top Christian Albums chart (dated April 17) at No. 3. All six songs concurrently reach the Hot Christian Songs chart, which is powered by airplay, sales and streaming data, likewise marking Bieber's first entries on the survey."[1]

William Ayles, D.D.

Freedom

Songwriters: Anderson Hernandez / Chris Kim / Jordan Douglas / Justin Drew Bieber / Matthew Jehu Samuels / Tyshane Thompson
Performed by Justin Bieber & BEAM
https://www.youtube.com/watch?v=FzpiRUWUdyk

Related Thoughts

In the article titled, "Justin Bieber's Testimony on finding Christianity," Megan Bailey writes:

"To the surprise of many, in recent year's pop megastar Justin Bieber has become increasingly open about his Christian faith. The once certified bad boy of Hollywood has taken a turn for the better, allowing Christ to come into his life and transform him.

"His testimony, though at first might seem a bit unrelatable, is actually one all Christians can learn from. While most of us have not grown up under the spotlight of Hollywood, most of us have gone through periods in our life where we didn't have it all together.

"Bieber was able to find Jesus when he needed Him the most. It's a powerful reminder that God is going to be by anyone's side, no matter whom they are or where they have come from.

"Bieber's baptism.

"In just one night it seemed like everything had caught up to the young star. Bieber felt that he had hit rock bottom; the drugs, tabloids, and women all were too much.

"It was 2014 and Bieber was staying with Carl Lentz, pastor of Hillsong Church, New York. Lentz began talking to Bieber after an introduction from a West Coast pastor, Judah Smith. Though Bieber was surrounded for years by Christian leaders, he hadn't been listening to their message, at least not at first.

"As Bieber sobbed on his knees of Lentz' apartment, he finally reached out and admitted that he needed Jesus. The two of them prayed together. It was then that Bieber ... asked for Lentz to baptize him. Lentz initially wanted to find a date [and] a time for the occasion, but Bieber knew that he wanted it to happen right then and there.

"'The choices he had made — he got to a place where he was like, "I want to start fresh."'" Lentz says.

"With the paparazzi circling the two it was hard to find a place to perform the ceremony at first.

"'We went to four different places,' Lentz says. 'I finally called my buddy Tyson Chandler.'

"Chandler, a professional basketball player living in New York at the time, received the phone call from Lentz around 3 a.m. 'I'm like, "Yeah, I need to borrow your [rooftop] pool,"' Lentz says. 'He's like, "I can't get into the pool, but come and use my bathtub."'

"Chandler, being over seven feet tall, had a tub that was large enough to baptize Bieber. Chandler's wife Kim got out food and drinks for the occasion, and placed towels around the tub. Though it was in the early morning hours, the baptism was … powerful and gave the star a new view of the world. The group gathered and prayed with Bieber as his life transformed.

"Growing up as a child star.

"After being discovered on YouTube in the late 2000s, Bieber blew up what felt like overnight. Bieber's 'Baby' became one of the most popular music videos ever and shot him right into the public eye. Millions of young teens swooned over the new star, while others bashed him outright.

"Unsurprisingly, Bieber found it difficult to adjust to his heightened profile, quickly going off the rails and hitting tabloid front pages on a regular basis for teenage pranks, drugs, turning up late for gigs or smashing up sports cars. He followed in the footsteps of many young troubled stars. However, [he] was 'still unfulfilled,' despite all the money, awards and fame.

"'I started doing pretty heavy drugs at 19 and abused all my relationships,' Bieber wrote in an Instagram post. 'I became resentful, disrespectful to women... hiding behind a shell of a person that I had become.'

"Bieber grew up in a Christian home, but like many Christians that faith was really one that was from his parents.

"'He has had a relationship with Jesus, and his mom did a great job doing her best to plant the right seeds. But you can get to a point as a man where it goes from being your mama's relationship... to yours,' Lentz says.

"Bieber's mother also went through some tough times. As a young adult, she was considering suicide. She found out a few months later that she was pregnant with Justin. Unmarried and afraid of how she ruined her own life, she at first was scared to turn to the church.

"When she did, though, they taught her the love of Christ. It was then she decided she was going to raise Justin to know Him too. She dedicated his life at a church in Ontario and took him on mission trips and to Toronto Blessing revival meetings. This gave the foundation for Justin to find God later on in his life. "Looking to the future.

"For the last few years, the singer has attended services by the Hillsong Church regularly and has even begun leading a few services. Despite what he went through growing up, he has now found peace with Jesus.

"'I felt like I could never turn it around,' he said. 'It's taken me years to bounce back from all these terrible decisions, fix broken relationships, and change relationship habits.'

"He got married to Hailey Baldwin, who also supports his Christian faith. The pair decided to remain celibate until they got married.

"'I wanted to rededicate myself to God in that way, because I really felt it was better for the condition of my soul,' Bieber told *Vogue*. 'And I believe that God blessed me with Hailey as a result. There are perks. You get rewarded for good behavior.'

"Now, Justin is happier, healthier, and stronger than ever because of his faith.

"'Luckily God blessed me with extraordinary people who love me for me,' Bieber said, adding that the 'best season' of his life, marriage, is teaching him 'patience, trust, commitment, kindness, humility, and all of the things it looks like to be a good man.'

"'I am set free from bondage and shame, I am a child of the most high God and he loves me exactly where I am, how I am, for who I am.'"[2]

Back in the late 1970s at UConn, I was searching for absolute truth. Unknown to me, that search would lead to my own freedom: the same "Freedom" Bieber is singing about.

To paint a picture of my mind at UConn, I'd like to quote what I wrote in my book, Treasures in Heaven. The Prologue begins as follows:

"Eternity...

This concept captured my attention a long time ago.

I had questions.

Why am I here?

What is my purpose?

What happens after I die?

How do I "get" to God?

How will I spend eternity?

"These are the questions that kept me awake at night during my senior year in college (1980). The obvious problem with asking and pondering these questions is that you need answers—and answers did follow.

"I attended an on-campus Bible study and I learned this: God is relevant. I realized—and felt—what Jesus of Nazareth said: 'Then you will know the truth, and the truth will set you free.'"[3]

1. https://www.billboard.com/pro/justin-biebermakes-top-christian-albums-chart-first-time/. Retrieval date: August 24, 2023.
2. https://www.beliefnet.com/entertainment/celebri ties/justin-biebers-testimony-on-findingchristianity.aspx. Retrieval date: July 9, 2023.
3. William Ayles, *Treasures in Heaven*, (TimeLine International, Inc., 2017), p. 5.

15   The Power of Prayer

In the article titled, "Bruce Springsteen's Relationship with Faith as He Insists Jesus Remains One of His Fathers," Oyin Balogun writes:

"When it comes to being a devotee to Jesus, the singer is determined not to go astray. Most notably, Bruce strives to maintain a personal relationship with Jesus, whom he refers to as one of his fathers, albeit, the supreme one.

"The 71-year-old, despite rejecting the concept of religion at an earlier age, has managed to create a balance between the catholic doctrine and his belief. In *Born To Run* [the Springsteen Memoir], the music legend admitted to believing in Jesus' power to save and to love."[1]

William Ayles, D.D.

In the article titled, "Bruce Springsteen's Letter to You: A Masterful Exploration of Faith, Death, and Life After Death," Wade Bearden writes:

"[I]n Springsteen's twentieth studio release, <u>Letter to You</u>, a propulsive, rock n' rollercoaster of an album that could only be written by someone who spent the better part of five decades trotting beside the mysterious practices of the Catholic Church. The sound fills rooms, and Springsteen employs his working man lyricism to craft a set of tunes submerged in the earthly, saintly, and holy. The album's <u>title track</u> itself frames the entire project as one long prayer—akin to a modern-day book of Psalms."[2]

Released in 2020, Letter to You contains the song,

THE POWER OF PRAYER

Songwriter: Bruce Springsteen
Performed by Bruce Springsteen & The E Street Band
https://www.youtube.com/watch?v=rZp8csyUi6w

Related Thoughts

I have a story about prayer and divine intervention...

Early in February 2000, I watched a movie on Martin Luther, who was a central figure during the Reformation of the 1500s. In one scene, Luther placed his right hand on the Bible while being "sworn in" as a Doctor of Theology.

Immediately, something deep within my soul stirred. I said aloud, "That would be the ultimate." Meaning... that would be the ultimate place for me in life: to be granted that type of divine liberty to search out the truths in the Scriptures. Simply stated, in that moment of the movie, I was spontaneously transparent.

> I didn't realize it at the time, but my spontaneous statement was actually a prayer. I said aloud what my soul cried out for.

When our souls cry aloud, that's prayer. And Christ answered that prayer. Just a few weeks later, He intervened in my life—and opened my eyes to see another (deeper) dimension of the spiritual realm. (See the Epilogue.)

In essence, Christ lifted the veil between the spiritual and material worlds. By doing so, Christ freed me from the limiting constraints of my mind—and granted me divine liberty to follow my prayer. And then, I took a deep dive into the Scriptures. The best way I know how to describe the impact of His intervention in 2000 is this:

> Christ was at the train station of life—and when my train arrived on February 24, 2000, He pulled the switch, and changed the track of my life. That day is forever etched in my mind as the onset of a different trajectory. That's how I arrived where I am now. Looking back, I see the prayer that preceded all of this.

Regarding prayer, Christ gave us insight on what it means to pour out our souls. Jesus spoke of useful prayers versus useless prayers:

> "And when you pray, do not be like the hypocrites, for they love to pray standing in the synagogues and on the street corners to be seen by others. Truly I tell you, they have received their reward in full. But when you pray, go into your room [inner chamber], close the door and pray to your Father, who is

unseen. Then your Father, who sees what is done in secret, will reward you."4

1. **https://news.amomama.com/251850-brucespringsteens-relationship-faith-he.html. Retrieval date: August 23, 2023.**
2. **https://christandpopculture.com/brucespringsteens-letter-to-you-a-masterfulexploration-of-faith-death-and-life-after-death/.**
   Retrieval date: August 23, 2023.
3. **https://brucespringsteen.net/. Retrieval date:**
   August 23, 2023.
4. **Matthew 6:5, 6.**

William Ayles, D.D.

16 Sweet Sounds of Heaven

In 2023, The Rolling Stones released Hackney Diamonds. The second single on the album is "Sweet Sounds of Heaven."[1]

In the 2023 article titled, "How the Rolling Stones Finally Got It Together and Made a Great New Album," Kory Grow writes:

"LAST YEAR, MICK Jagger started feeling restless. Seventeen years had passed since the Rolling Stones had released an album of original material, and though they'd toured regularly — and made the difficult choice to soldier on after the devastating 2021 death of drummer Charlie Watts — the on-and-off sessions they'd held for a potential new LP over the past decade hadn't produced much they could use. When the Stones' tour ended in Berlin last August, Jagger decided he'd had enough. So he pulled Keith Richards aside.

"'I told Keith, "I think some of the tracks are good, but most of them are not as good as they should be,"' Jagger recalls on a phone call from Italy. "'I think we should give ourselves a deadline [to finish the album], and then we should go out and tour the album." And then he looked at me, and he said, "Yeah, OK. That sounds like what we used to do."' Jagger pauses and laughs. 'I'm sure Keith would tell a completely different story.'

"The record's guest list reads like popular music's Hall of Presidents: Paul McCartney, Stevie Wonder, Elton John, Lady Gaga, and even self-exiled Stones bassist Bill Wyman, who returned for one of Watts' final recordings.

"Moving forward without Charlie Watts, one of rock & roll's all-time great drummers, was far from easy. 'Anything I do is a tribute to Charlie Watts,' Richards says. 'It's impossible for me to lay anything down without automatically thinking that Mr. Watts is laying the backbeat down.' Watts' presence on the album was important to the Stones. 'If you've got Charlie Watts on it, man, that's it,' Richards exclaims. 'I so miss that, man.'

"As they worked, they also started welcoming guests into the studio — including an old friend and fellow legend: Stevie Wonder, who helped to summon a vibe on the gospel-ish 'Sweet Sounds of Heaven.'

"Before they started recording, Wonder and the Stones talked a little about the old days (Wonder says he took the energy from the road then into the studio when he recorded 'Superstition'), and they jammed on a jazzy version of 'Satisfaction,' and then on a reggae version. Then they got down to business. Wonder played traditional piano, Fender Rhodes, and Moog bass on 'Heaven.'

"'I felt that the song needed a place of celebration, a celebration of the spirit of the rhythms and the spirit of just everybody coming together for that event,' Wonder says, adding how he was moved by the way in which the song paid tribute to Watts. 'It's not saying, "Goodbye," to me, it's saying, "Hello."'"[2]

SWEET SOUNDS OF HEAVEN

William Ayles, D.D.

Songwriters: Michael Phillip Jagger / Keith Richards
Performed by The Rolling Stones & Lady Gaga
https://www.youtube.com/watch?v=YEJd5xtbEPY

Related Thoughts

In the 2001 article titled, "Person of the Year: Mick Jagger," David Fricke quoted Mick Jagger. Jagger said:

"I have a spiritual side. Everyone has one. It's whether they're going to lock it up or not. Our lives are so busy that we never get any time to be, first, reflective, then afterward, to let some sort of spiritual light into your life. But there are moments in your life when that appears.

I've written about it before – touched on it in odd songs like 'I Just Want to See His Face' and 'Shine a Light' [both on 1972's *Exile on Main Street*]. 'Joy' is more fleshed out. It is about the joy of creation, inspiring you to a love of God."[3]

In the 2015 article titled, "Keith Richards' secret to immortality," Bang Showbiz states:

"He [Richards] said: 'There's nobody in my family that ever had anything to do with organized religion.... Thank God, otherwise Sundays would have been even more boring than they were....'

"The guitarist was asked by a fan during the band's first ever Twitter Q&A what he thinks the secret to living forever is and gave his tips. "When asked the question, he responded: 'I ain't there yet! So far so good. I think a clean and healthy life, plenty of exercise, go to church on a Sunday.'

"He added: 'Spirit is all around me. Very much. That's why I did the "Wingless Angels" album: very spiritual music. But mine is a very nebulous spirituality. I wouldn't care to put a name on it. I wouldn't want to place any bets. Religion is too much like Las Vegas. "Oh, you've picked the wrong God." ... I prefer to take the larger point of view.'"4

"Sweet Sounds of Heaven"

Jagger and Richards—in a tribute to their drummer— created a motion picture of truth: There is a sweet connection between Heaven and Earth—that ever flows.

The ever-flowing connection between Heaven and Earth takes on several forms—which includes the Spirit of Truth. Christ pours out this Spirit from Heaven, and it fills our soul as a fountain of spiritual life. Jesus said:

> "'If anyone is thirsty, let him come to Me and drink. He who believes in Me, as the Scripture has said, out of his heart shall flow rivers of living water.' By this He spoke of the Spirit [of Truth], whom those who believe in Him
> would receive."[5]

"Sweet Sounds of Heaven" and "living water" have striking similarities...

In "Sweet Sounds of Heaven," Jagger sings of quenching his thirst—and not going to hell. With "living water," the Spirit is given to those who thirst (for spiritual truth)—and the Spirit is the key to the "stairway." Thus, in a spiritual sense, Jesus Christ and Mick Jagger are speaking with one mind:

> Quenching our spiritual thirst brings forth a different destination, Heaven.

When the Spirit fills our flesh and blood, we are no longer just body and soul, but rather, body, soul, and Spirit—and Heaven awaits. The apostle Paul also made this connection:

> [A]fter hearing the word of truth, the gospel of your salvation, and after

believing in Him, were sealed with the promised Holy Spirit, who is the guarantee of our [heavenly] inheritance.[6]

1. https://therollingstonesshop.com/products/sweetsounds-of-heaven-10-vinyl. Retrieval date: November 9, 2023.
2. https://www.rollingstone.com/music/musicfeatures/rolling-stones-mick-jagger-keith-richardshackney-diamonds-stevie-wonder-1234822701/.
Retrieval date: November 7, 2023.
3. https://www.rollingstone.com/music/musicnews/people-of-the-year-mick-jagger-246297/. Retrieval date: May 24, 2024.
4. https://www.azcentral.com/story/entertainment/people/2015/05/19/keith-richards-secretimmortality/27575133/. May 24, 2024.
5. John 7:37–39.
6. Ephesians 1:13, 14.

William Ayles, D.D.

17   Get Together

In 1967, The Youngbloods covered and released "Get Together." The lead singer of The Youngbloods—Jesse Colin Young—sat down with the Professor of Rock and they recalled the (unique) re-creation of this song.

Young said, "This was angelic work; just angels pushing me in the right direction."[1]

William Ayles, D.D.

In the 2019 article titled, "Beyond The Summer Of Love, 'Get Together' Is An Anthem For Every Season," Tom Cole writes:

"In 1967, the Vietnam War was raging. The Youngbloods' lead singer, Jesse Colin Young, remembers, 'Back then we were all subject to the draft. That made everything more life and death. And hope is what comes out of that song.'

"The band [The Youngbloods] rehearsed in Greenwich Village's Café au Go Go when there wasn't a show happening, and that's where Young first heard 'Get Together.' 'That song just stopped me in my tracks.'

"Young says it was the lyrics that really grabbed him. '"Love is but a song we sing / Fear's the way we die." Wow — the human condition in two lines.'

"Though it ['Get Together'] didn't get much national attention in 1967, two years later The Youngbloods' version was used in a public service announcement for the National Conference of Christians and Jews. People started calling their radio stations requesting the song.

"The Youngbloods' version of 'Get Together' went to

No. 5 on *Billboard*'s Hot 100 chart. [Ben] Fong Torres [music journalist] says it captured the zeitgeist of the time, albeit in a roundabout way: 'It took a band from New York City to give San Francisco and the Haight-Ashbury generation its anthem.'

"One meaning of the word 'anthem' is a psalm or hymn. 'Get Together' definitely carries that message for Young, who was a born-again Christian in his teens. And Young says it still carries a message — for our times.

"'Every night I sing it, it's my favorite part of the show because the people sing,' he says. 'I played it in Central Park this past summer, and that was on the first anniversary of Charlottesville. Those people sang it stronger than I've ever heard it sung. Some people were pumping their fists, and I
realized they were saying, "We choose love."'"[2]

In the "Rock History Music" interview titled, "'Get Together' The Story Behind The 60s Iconic Classic Via Jesse Colin Young – Youngbloods," John Beaudin spoke with Jesse Colin Young about the origin of his experience with the song. Young said:

"I'm in [Greenwich] village…. It's Sunday afternoon. I'm thinking, oh, I'll go by [the Café au Go Go] and check it out.

William Ayles, D.D.

"So, it's two flights down from Bleeker [Street]. And I get to the first flight, and I said, 'oh man there's music.' And for some reason, instead of turning around [hoping for an empty stage to rehearse], I walked down the second flight. I hit the landing. Buzzy Linhart is on stage singing 'Get Together.' [And] just like in those movies about the Bible, I mean… the heavens opened, and I really had an epiphanal experience. I knew my life had changed and I knew that this was my path."[3]

The Youngbloods put their stamp on it, and "Get Together" became an iconic classic—another anthem for love. It is pure joy to sing.

GET TOGETHER

Songwriter: Chester William Jr. Powers (a.k.a. Dino Valenti)
Performed by The Youngbloods
https://www.youtube.com/watch?v=o7CTovI-DZg

Related Thoughts

Going back to the life and times of Jesus Christ...

He came into our world with a fundamental purpose: to light the torch of divine truth, so we could be drawn to Him and turn our hearts and lives to divine light and love. He lived it.

He also taught in parables—including the parable of the "Good Samaritan." This story draws upon, "Love your neighbor as yourself." Then, a lawyer asked Jesus a question:

"And who is my neighbor?"

"Jesus answered, 'A man went down from Jerusalem to Jericho and fell among thieves, who stripped him of his clothing and wounded him and departed, leaving him half dead. By chance a [temple] priest came down that way. And when he saw him, he passed by on the other side. So likewise a Levite [temple authority], when he came to that place, looked at him and passed by on the other side. But a Samaritan, as he journeyed, came where he was. And when he saw him, he had compassion on him, and went to him and bound up his wounds, pouring in oil and wine. Then he set him on his own donkey and brought him to an inn, and took care of him. The next day when he departed, he took out two denarii and gave them to the innkeeper and said to him, "Take care of him. I will repay you whatever else you spend when I return."'

"'Now which of these three do you think was a neighbor to him who fell among the thieves?' He [the lawyer] said, 'The one who showed mercy on him.' Then Jesus said to him, 'Go and do likewise.'"[4]

1. https://www.youtube.com/watch?v=mPKFIC8no Ck. Retrieval date: January 17, 2024.
2. https://www.npr.org/2019/04/10/711545679/gettogether-youngbloods-summer-of-love-americananthem. Retrieval date: January 18, 2024.
3. https://www.youtube.com/watch?v=e2OcLHgNoJ c&t=5s. Retrieval date: January 18, 2024.
4. Luke 10:27, 29–37.

Don't Fear the Reaper

18
It's the End of the World as We Know It (And I Feel Fine)

Released in 1987, the R.E.M. album Document included the song, "It's the End of the World as We Know It (And I Feel Fine)."[1]

In the article titled, "REM – It's the End of the World as We Know It (And I Feel Fine)," Michael Stipe [of R.E.M.] spoke about the song's origin:

"'The words come from everywhere. I'm extremely aware of everything around me, whether I am in a sleeping state, awake, dream-state or just in day-today life.... It's a collection of streams of consciousness.'

"Stipe claims to have a lot of dreams about the end of the world, destroyed buildings and the like. His stream-of-consciousness writing style in this [song] is very similar to the way a dream moves."[2]

It's the End of the World as We Know It (And I Feel Fine)

Songwriters: John Michael Stipe / Michael E. Mills / Peter Lawrence Buck / William Thomas Berry
Performed by R.E.M.
https://www.youtube.com/watch?v=9p3LXWokQCY

Related Thoughts

I have been playing this song on my back deck for the last few years; the "vibe" of the song resonates with my soul.

While writing this book, I finally decided to look at the lyrics—and I was stunned: I never knew the lyrics spoke of the "Rapture" and being "saved." The Rapture is a stairway to Heaven. Thus, there is cause to revel in the truth—and to know the effect of feeling "fine."

During The Last Supper, Christ issued a prophecy of the Rapture:

"Let not your heart be troubled. You believe in God. Believe also in Me. In My Father's house are many dwelling places. If it were not so, I would have told you. I am going to prepare a place for you. And if I go and prepare a place for you, I will come again and receive you to Myself, that where I am [Heaven], you may be also [Heaven]."[3]

The Rapture will happen at a dramatic moment in time: "the day of the Lord."[4] And R.E.M. is right: That "day" does begin with an "earthquake." The Rapture becomes a reality at the sixth seal of the Book of Revelation:

"I [John] watched as he opened the sixth seal. There was a great earthquake. The sun turned black like sackcloth made of goat hair, the whole moon turned blood red, and the stars in the sky fell to earth, as figs drop from a fig tree when shaken by a strong wind. The heavens receded like a scroll being rolled up, and every mountain and island was removed from its place."[5]

When will this prophecy be fulfilled? Regarding God's timeline, Christ Himself foretold of a generation that will experience these end-time events... and we are that generation. (See the Epilogue.) There is no glory found in taking the "head in the sand" approach to time. Going back in time, Christ upbraided those in the crowd who were blissfully unaware of God's timetable:

> "Then He said to the crowd: 'When you see a cloud rise out of the west, immediately you say, "A shower is coming," and so it is. And when a south wind blows, you say, "There will be heat," and it happens. You hypocrites! You can discern the face of the sky and of the earth. But why do you not know how to discern this time?'"[6]

1. https://remhq.com.Retrieval:September 12, 2023.
2. https://powerpop.blog/2018/12/01/rem-its-theend-of-the-world-as-we-know-it-and-i-feel-fine/. Retrieval: September 10, 2023.
3. John 14:1–3.
4. Acts 2:20; 1 Thess. 5:2; Rev. 6:17; Zeph. 1:14, 15.
5. Revelation 6:12–14.
6. Luke 12:54–56.

19 Backstage

The following 3 musicians speak of their arrival.

Donna Summer

In the 2022 article titled, "Donna Summer: 'I was filled by God's Holy Spirit and gloriously born again,'" a *Movieguide* ® contributor writes:

"Most people remember Donna Summer for her disco hits, but did you know the star was also a devout Christian?

"Summer's father was a pastor and the singer said she first heard God's voice when she was just ten years old. Summer had just finished singing a solo in her church choir when she heard an 'inner voice.' 'It sort of knocked everybody out of the pews,' Summer said. 'When I looked up through my tears, everyone in the whole church's eyes were downcast and they were crying, and I thought, "Oh my God." I looked at my dad and he was crying.'

"'It was that, on that first time I ever sang, that I heard God speak to me, and He said to me that I was gonna be famous,' the singer explained.

'And that I was not to misuse the power that He was giving me.'

"Summer rose to fame in the 1970s on the strength of disco hits like 'I Feel Love' and 'Bad Girls,' but fame took a toll on the star. She returned to her faith in 1979 and recommitted herself to God. 'I was finally filled by God's Holy Spirit and gloriously born again,' Summer said of her return to faith.

"'I never stopped being a Christian,' the star explained. 'Being born-again is an affirmation that the person is going to make a personal effort to walk closer to God and bring Him into one's life and start following His way.'

"'There are parts in your life where you can look back and laugh: "I can't believe I did that; how could I have said that; where's my head at?"' Summer continued. 'I'm sad that all the running I did was only running; it didn't get me anywhere. The spirit of rebellion in myself and in my songs would not let me rest. But I've chosen to stay in the world's eye, to give a positive image. It's a very spiritual and a very helpful place to
be. I love it.'"[1]

Dave Mustaine

In the 2009 article titled, "Onward Christian Soldier: Megadeth's Dave Mustaine talks of his spiritual reinvention," Steve Wildsmith writes:

"As bandleader of Megadeth since 1983, he [Dave Mustaine] had released one album after another that continually put him in the top tier of rock 'n' roll guitar players. He had toured the world, performing to a generation of headbanging young people who awaited the release of every new record like Moses taking those first stone tablets from God.

"He swam in a sea of booze, indulged in every conceivable form of sexual excess and smoked, snorted, shot up and gobbled every substance both legal and illicit. But in 2002, it all seemed to come to an abrupt end when an accident left him unable to even make a fist with his left hand, much less pick up a guitar – and Dave Mustaine found himself spiritually, emotionally and mentally destitute.

"And then he found God.

"For fans who associate the ferocity and brutality of Megadeth's brand of speed metal with doom and darkness, such a profound conversion by Mustaine was earth-shattering. But, Mustaine told *The Daily Times* during a recent interview, his own world was already shattered, and becoming a Christian was the one way he's found to put the pieces back together.

"'There was a moment of reckoning when my arm was destroyed, and I was up on this hill, and there was a cross at the top of it,' Mustaine said. 'It was just one of those thoughts – I was baptized a Lutheran, brought up as a Jehovah's Witness, got into witchcraft and Satanism and practicing black magic. My wife was in another thing, and I was thinking that was a cult, so I'd gone back to being a Jehovah's Witness, but I wasn't happy.'

"'Looking up at that cross, I said six simple words – "What have I got to lose?" And my whole life has changed. It's been hard, but I wouldn't change it for anything. I'd rather... go my whole life believing that there is a God and find out there isn't than live my whole life thinking there isn't a God and then find out, when I die, that there is.'

"Not only did Mustaine convert to Christianity, he made a full recovery – even though doctors told him he would never play guitar again, today he's ranked as the No. 1 greatest metal guitarist in the world by author and metal auteur Joel McIver."[2]

"I got saved. I'm a born-again Christian."[3] — Dave Mustaine

Lou Gramm

In the article titled, "Top 10 Rockers Who Found God," Andy Greene writes:

"In the late 1990s Foreigner frontman Lou Gramm suffered a benign brain tumor. In one of rock's most bizarre ironies, his first symptom was actually double vision. He emerged from the experience a changed man, and soon after quit Foreigner and embraced Jesus. When fans see his solo show they get a bizarre mix of Foreigner hits and Christian rock songs."[4]

In the article titled, "Lou Gramm: Foreigner's lead singer talks about becoming a Christian," Gramm spoke to the editor of *HM Magazine*, Doug Van Pelt. Van Pelt interviewed Gramm for the July/August 1996 issue of *HM Magazine*.

"Doug: 'Every Christian has their own story about how they came to Christ. What's your story?'

"Lou: 'Well, I'll try to make it as brief as possible. I really have always felt the presence of the Lord, and certainly acknowledged him, but always seemed to keep him at arm's length and only called upon him when I needed him....

William Ayles, D.D.

I think I just came to a point in my life where, as a parent and just as a person, I had really emotionally and spiritually bottomed out. I just felt there was more to life, certainly, than what I was getting out of it. I could see not only the state and the condition of this world and the country we live in, but my own personal life and my beliefs and everything were just needed to call out to him and ask for something meaningful – to put everything in perspective. I feel there's more to it than the amount of time we have on this planet.'

"Doug: 'What was the timetable when this was happening?'

"Lou: 'I think really over the last dozen years, maybe from the mid-'80s. I think the material success and the public accolades and just the whole celebrity thing – I never bought into it, and I was always uncomfortable with it. I just knew that it wasn't the part that I was in this career for. For me, it was for the creative end of it and really being able to reach people through the songs I was writing and performing. But, all the other stuff that went along with it kind of diminished my enthusiasm for what I was doing.'

"'So, I would say that through the mid '80s, late '80s, and early '90s, I was on the fringe… I was doing some shopping, spiritual shopping. I got an earful and an education about New Age spirituality, etc. That left me cold. I really was searching in those years. Through the years, some very dear friends of mine began to attend a non-denominational church in Rochester.'

"'I really found what I was looking for: a real "come as you are" type of attitude, really steeped in the Word, and the Scriptures and the teachings that are applicable to today's life and the world that we're living in now. I really got into the book of Revelation. I just found what I was looking for – a real sense of well being in being a follower of Jesus. I think that everything I had been through up to that point in my life led me up to where I finally made the commitment and accepted him as my Lord and my Saviour, instead of just a part time, "get me out of trouble" God. I think that's where the difference lies. That's kind of it in a nutshell.'

"Doug: 'I remember hearing about the experience you guys had when filming the video to "I Want To Know What Love Is", where the New Jersey Mass Choir came in, and everyone held hands and repeated the Lord's Prayer...'

"Lou: 'Yeah, that was actually during the recording, not the video. They did that before they sang on the recording and it was really moving. It stunned us in the control room. We were just literally moved to tears that their performance was directed at our Lord. I think anyone could feel that the song goes way beyond a love ballad. I think emotionally, I was turned inside out and emptied out.'

"Doug: 'Have you imagined in your mind, or formulated a vision of what it must be like for God the Father when you are singing unto him?'

"Lou: 'Well, I hope he's smiling. I'm not sure. He's all knowing, so he certainly knows what's going on. He knows my thoughts and my heart. I try and keep it pure and focused when I sing. For me, now, it's a lot different than in years past, but I still have fun with it. It's quite a bit more meaningful now than it ever has been. I thank him for the gift that he's given me, and I maintain a sense of humility about it and acknowledge that it is a gift from him and it's not my skill or my good fortune. I'm blessed.'"[5]

On November 28, 1978...

Foreigner came to the New Haven Coliseum in Connecticut. I took a lovely lady, Laurie, from my UConn dorm.

Foreigner was phenomenal—and she was too. That night remains in my memory a unique moment in time because of what I felt: overwhelming love for the first time in my life for a woman. OMG.

At that time, Foreigner broke into the radio waves with their big hit, "Feels Like the First Time." I could relate. Yet, the story with Laurie went nowhere. But I learned something about myself: I had an obvious inability to translate love into a meaningful relationship. Nevertheless, the love I felt was real. And I knew I had to bring it back into my life—somehow.

And this story brings me to another story: There was another woman in my dorm, Susan, who attended an on-campus Bible study group. She was not typical. She radiated love, peace, and joy. At first, I thought this couldn't be real. I was skeptical.

Yet, I came to a life-changing conclusion: Only the truth could have produced the love she radiated. My conclusion about Susan dawned on me during my own personal drama: All those "eternal" questions (found in Chapter 14) swirled in my head. These same questions caused me to lose sleep... which caused me to question everything. And on top of that, I'm looking back and lamenting over losing love. Geesh...

In January 1980, all those eternal questions came crashing down in my mind.

January is the UConn winter break. I'm between my seventh and eighth semesters. I'm living at home, working at a grocery store. I stocked shelves. And, during one frigid January afternoon, I arrived at the store for work. I was assigned to the dog-food aisle. And that's exactly how I felt: *like dog food.*

I remember that night. While stocking the shelves, I slammed a can of dog food down on my metal cart, and I said aloud: "When I get back to UConn, I'm going to see Susan."

William Ayles, D.D.

I had an epiphany:

The answer to my ongoing search—to find absolute truth—had been staring me... right in the face: Susan lived divine love and the truth. I didn't know it at the time, but she was filled with the Spirit of Truth.

1. https://www.movieguide.org/newsarticles/donna-summer-i-was-filled-by-gods-holyspirit-and-gloriously-born-again.html#:~:text=She%20returned%20to%20her%20faith,Christian%2C%E2%80%9D%20the%20 star%20explained. Retrieval date: July 23, 2023.
2. https://rockgod.co.nz/id192.htm Retrieval date: July 10, 2023.
3. https://www.johnrothra.com/entertainment/musi c/mustaine-i-got-saved-im-a-born-againchristian/. Retrieval: July 10, 2023.
4. https://www.rollingstone.com/music/musiclists/top-10-rockers-who-found-god-20985/lougramm-240841/. Retrieval date: July 10, 2023.
5. https://www.crossrhythms.co.uk/articles/music/L ou_Gramm_Foreigners_lead_singer_talks _about _becoming_a_Christian/40555/p1/. Retrieval date: July 10, 2023.

Epilogue: Divine Intervention

God's initial intervention in my life occurred in 1980.

I found that candle in that cave...

Now, continuing with my story from the last chapter...

I'm done stocking shelves in the grocery store.

It's late January.

I'm back at UConn.

So is Susan, but she had moved to a different dorm.

I walked across the frozen tundra of the UConn campus, found her dorm room, and knocked on her door.

She was surprised to see me.

Immediately I said, "Susan, what makes you this way?"

She said, "I'm blessed. Come on in."

We sat cross-legged on the floor and talked about eternity. Then, she played a song by a Christian group. As I listened to the song, I melted. I heard divine truth, in a song.

Then, I decided to attend her on-campus Bible study.

There, I understood—for the first time in my life—the mystery revealed to the apostle Paul: We become sons of the living God by faith; we enter the kingdom of God by faith; we receive God's righteousness by faith... by believing and confessing the message of faith. Paul said:

> "This is the word [message] of faith that we preach: that if you confess with your mouth Jesus is Lord, and believe in your heart that God has raised Him from the dead, you will be saved, for with the heart one believes unto righteousness, and with the mouth confession is made unto salvation."[1]

I declared Christ as *my* Lord.
In other words, I decided I'm no longer lord of my own life.
And that was fine with me.
Whoever spoke as Jesus Christ?
I believed Him when He said:

> "I am the light of the world. Whoever follows Me shall not walk in the darkness, but shall have the light of life."[2]

I opened the door of my heart to Christ *the Lord.* As Bono revealed earlier in the book, he drew upon C.S. Lewis in Mere Christianity: "Jesus had to be a lunatic, liar or Lord." Bono picked Lord. So did I. I declared what was declared 2000 years ago:

> "Yes, Lord, I believe that You are the Christ, the Son of God, who is to come into the world."[3]

I believed... and received God's righteousness.
I confessed... and received salvation: eternal life.
I broke open my soul and surrendered to Him.

Christ—as our High Priest—baptized me with the Spirit of Truth. This baptism became my reality when I turned to Him. He baptized me from Heaven!

I had new "spiritual life."
Now, absolute truth was within me—in Spirit form.
It is the arrival.
I became a partaker of God's divine nature: divine love.
"God is Spirit."[4]
"God is love."[5]
Both the Spirit and His love are not made of matter... *but both fill matter*... us. And, as I understood this concept of God's nature within, the following Scriptures really spoke to me:

"[Y]ou have been born again [anew], not from perishable seed, but imperishable [seed, the Spirit of Truth], through the word of God which lives and abides forever."[6]

"For God hath not given us the spirit of fear; but of power, and of love, and of a sound mind."[7]

"He [God] has delivered us from the power of darkness and has transferred us into the kingdom of His dear Son."[8]

By an act of God, I entered an eternal, spiritual kingdom in this world. I crossed a spiritual threshold in a moment of time. The kingdom of God was within me—which is eternal (and so are we). A miracle.

Christ filled me with His Spirit—and I knew this: Zero good works were needed to receive God's Spirit. Thank God. It is by faith.
Consider the question that Paul asked:

"Does God give you the Spirit and work miracles among you by the works of the law, or by hearing with faith?"[9]

By an act of God I was born anew. And this act of God cannot be reversed by the hand of man. The Spirit of Truth—the divine seed—cannot perish. The Spirit is with us forever.

And back in 1980...

Christ granted me a supernatural sign— which confirmed the presence of His Spirit within: I spoke forth a language of the Spirit—which Christ called "new tongues."[10] And with this divine sign, it became clear to me: There must be a stairway to Heaven.

Why?

If the words are true about the *effect* (receiving the Spirit and a divine sign), then the words must be true about the *cause*, Christ (who gives the Spirit and a divine sign).

And Christ guarantees a stairway to Heaven.

(To learn more about the sign of speaking in this divine language, see my publication, *Treasures in Heaven*, and see the article titled, "Divine Intervention: The Spirit" on my website, www.thetimeline.org.)

For me, when I spoke in a divine language, I could never, ever look back. And I realized this: I fulfilled a prophecy that Christ Himself issued on the day of His Ascension to Heaven.

"These signs will accompany those who believe: In My name… they will speak with new tongues."[11]

Consider this stunning truth: This sign of "new tongues" is a supernatural sign of Christ's Resurrection from the dead. For, the only way to speak forth a divine language, is by the Spirit of Truth. And the only way to be filled with the Spirit of Truth, is if Jesus Christ filled you with it. And the only way He could fill you with it, is if He was resurrected, and He ascended to the right hand of God.

With the Spirit of Truth within, Christ could now impart direct, divine revelation to my mind— which is a spiritual "gift" known as the "word of knowledge."[12]

All those years ago… I crossed the spiritual wall by embracing what was in my heart: eternity. And
here's my take on the matter…

To do the opposite—to not embrace eternity— is like fighting in a fight that's fixed: eternity is lost—forever.

"Jesus Christ Superstar"

Alice Cooper sang "King Herod's Song" in Jesus Christ Superstar. I placed this song in the

Epilogue because King Herod is *the* poster child for fighting in a fight that's fixed: He lost.

KING HEROD'S SONG

https://www.youtube.com/watch?v=9BnxwP8vLRg

In the article titled, "Alice Cooper on 'Jesus Christ Superstar' and His Bad Past," Tim Appelo interviewed Alice Cooper:

"Appelo: 'You're probably the No. 1 Christian rock star. Is it weird to play Herod, who hates Jesus?'

"Cooper: 'I'm going to be persecuting Jesus Christ, whom I worship. I actually prayed about it, and I realized it was absolutely no problem. It does really glorify Christ. And I have the funniest song in the whole show.'"[13]

William Ayles, D.D.

Six Divine Weeks: 2000

On the night of February 24, 2000, God intervened in my life.

And He forever changed my life.

From that first night, I experienced one supernatural event after another—for six straight weeks. Christ lifted the veil between the natural and spiritual realms. I could perceive the "other side." And down the "rabbit hole" I went.

Fantastical reality followed.

I *experienced* what the apostle Peter prophesied:

"'In the last days it shall be,' says God, 'that I will pour out My Spirit on all flesh; your sons and your daughters shall prophesy, your young men shall see visions, and your old men shall dream dreams.'"[14]

On that first night, I was sprawled out on the couch, having just returned from a business trip. At 8:00 p.m., I decided to watch a PBS special on Stonehenge (the circular stone structure in England). Twenty minutes into the show, the narrator posed questions about who built Stonehenge, suggesting possibly the Druids built it around the time of Christ.

I said out loud, "The Druids didn't build it; that survived the flood [meaning the flood of Noah]." (I was convinced the structure predated the time of Christ—and Noah. And when the waters of Noah's flood receded, Stonehenge remained.)

As soon as I said, "that survived the flood," God flooded my entire being with supernatural energy. Then, pictures of Creation filled my mind. Immediately, I knew this was divine revelation: direct knowledge from God.

For two solid hours, pictures of Creation and divine energy poured into me. After this two-hour internal movie came to an end, I saw a phrase in my mind: "generations of old."

The following night, I opened my *Strong's Concordance*, to see if "generations of old" appeared in Scripture. It does. It's in Isaiah 51, verse 9. I opened my *King James Bible*, and this is what I read:

> "Awake, awake, put on strength, O arm of the LORD; awake, as in the ancient days, in the generations of old."[15]

What?!

God spoke to me... me... through the prophet Isaiah: "Awake, awake, put on strength"!

God gave me a wakeup call!

Time to put on strength.

Time to put on Scripture.

Time to dive into His Word with His blessing.

Awake!

These first two nights of intervention set the stage for the mind-expanding, divine events that followed. On one night, while sitting cross-legged on the couch, I experienced a stunning phenomenon: In my mind, saw my Holy Spirit lift out of my body.

I saw the form of the Spirit.

It appeared in the same shape as my physical being.

Then, out of nowhere, I saw a vision of a fireball coming straight down out of Heaven—filling me. I knew the fireball was a Spirit—replacing the Spirit that had just risen from me.

As the fireball descended into my being, I spoke supernaturally: I spoke out loud a declaration about my relationship with my Lord Christ. I repeated this declaration 3 times.

It *floored* me.

(If Christ again intervenes in my life and directs me to disclose what He gave me to say, I will.)

When I spoke supernaturally, God transformed my own sense of who I am. I could never—nor would I ever—think the same.

How could I?

Finally, on the last day of His intervention, April 6, God gave me a thought: "Go outside at 8:00 p.m., and look up at the sky." (At this time of the year in Connecticut, it is dusk, nearly dark.)

That evening, a thick blanket of grey clouds covered the sky.

Rain fell.

This drizzling rain continued to fall as I peered outside.

Obviously, the weather made it impossible to see the sky.

At 7:55 p.m. I went out, looked up, and decided to focus my attention on where the moon is positioned in the sky. Soon after my arrival outside, the rain stopped.

Moments later, a supernatural event occurred:

> *A cloud—shaped like a blimp—broke away from the rest of the clouds, opening a hole in the sky, revealing the heavens. I saw the moon and three planets, all in alignment. My jaw practically hit the pavement as my eyes fixated on this celestial alignment.*

Then the blimp-shaped cloud floated down to about a hundred feet over my head. I was gripped, watching this cloud while it continued floating; then it floated away. I turned my attention back to the moon, and the hole in the clouds slowly closed.

Supernaturally, God showed me a celestial alignment.

Why?

For many years, I had understood that heavenly bodies are set in motion by God to communicate His Word, His signs, and His timing.

Psalm 19 states:

> "The heavens declare the glory of God; the skies proclaim the work of his hands. Day after day they pour forth speech; night after night they reveal knowledge. They have no speech, they use no words; no sound is heard from them. Yet their voice goes out into all the earth, their words to the ends of the world."[16]

God spoke to me by the voice of the heavens.

This celestial alignment was a "hand" on God's "divine clock."

I sensed it meant time is of the essence. In other words, the time of the Rapture is on the horizon.

The next day, April 7, I researched celestial alignments. I realized God showed me the beginning of the alignment known as "The Grand Alignment."[17] This alignment would come together in totality on May 5, 2000. On that date, five planets—Mercury, Venus, Mars, Jupiter, and Saturn—would line up with the moon, Earth, and the sun.

That night, April 6, 2000, proved to be God's grand finale; it was the end of the phenomenal odyssey. God's intervention had lasted exactly six weeks—almost to the minute—after it started.

By way of this intervention, God answered that prayer of mine (given in Chapter

15): to be granted the God-given liberty to research His matchless Word.

Now, I have a story to relate.

During this intervention (2000), I took my sweetheart, Vera, out to dinner. I revealed the supernatural events taking place. I told her I would write a book. She said, "Honey, that's nice, write your book—just don't quit your job." I looked back at her and said, "I already did."

Amid God's intervention, I left the corporate world. Following the intervention, I moved out to a cottage by a lake and began researching and writing.

After decades of research, I continue to "see" the unmistakable: Only the mind of a divine Creator could have authored such a book as the Bible. As the apostle Peter said, "prophecy never had its origin in the human will, but prophets, though human, spoke from God as they were carried along by the Holy Spirit."[18]

I close this personal documentary with personal joy.

When Vera spoke of growing up in Russia, she spoke of the atheistic, political atmosphere: churches were museums. The politicians created their own walls between the population and spirituality.

And the news is...

Vera—once an atheist—recently opened her heart to Christ!

Listen to what she told me: "I felt a weight come off me.... For the first time in my life, I felt like I was not alone."

Our spiritual reality is this: The kingdom of God is within us now by faith, and the full expression of it (ultimately) is in Paradise, which goes on into... infinity.

"Stigmata"

Regarding this divine intervention of 2000, there is one movie that reflects what I experienced: "Stigmata" (minus the bloody wounds). I've watched the movie several times. I can easily relate to the main character. She experienced divine intervention—which opened a door to the spiritual dimension. My "door" differed from the movie. Yet, just like the main character, I could never think or be the same.

And in the movie, we hear something profound:

> "The kingdom of God is inside you, and all around you. Not in buildings of wood and stone. Split a piece of wood, and I am there. Lift a stone, and you will find Me."
>
> —The Gospel of Thomas (Discovered in 1945, it is written in the language of Jesus:

Aramaic.)

Christ: Our End Times

Finally, what did Christ say about the end times?
Where are we on God's timeline?
How do modern events in Israel figure into prophecy?
Listen to what Christ revealed about a future generation:

> "Now learn this lesson from the fig tree [Israel]: When its branch becomes tender and grows leaves, you know that summer is near. So also, when you shall see all these things, you know that it is near, even at the doors. Truly I say to you, this generation will not pass away until all these things take place."[19]

A "Generation"

After nearly 2000 years, Israel (the fig tree) was replanted in the Holy Land. (The "fig tree" is a symbol for Israel.)[20] In 1948, Israel declared its independence; the Jews have returned to their homeland. This marker in time—Israel's replanting— is Christ's first signal to us. This fulfilled "part 1" of His prophecy. This sets the stage for "part 2": end-time events to come to pass—in our generation.

Although the length of a "generation" (referred to by Christ) is debated, it is most likely either 70-80 years[21] or 120 years[22] (as given in the Old Testament). Regardless of our interpretation of a generation, we are that generation.[23]

Celestial Signs

The second signal Christ gave us revolves around celestial signs. He said, "There will be signs in the sun and the moon and the stars."[24] The rebirth of Israel coincided with the 1949-1950 lunar pattern, known as a "Tetrad": four consecutive total lunar eclipses (blood moons). And these blood moons—over the course of those 2 years—*fell on Jewish holy days.*

Then, in 1967, during the "Six-day War," the Jews recaptured "Old Jerusalem." This coincided with another Tetrad—which also fell on Jewish holy days: 1967-1968. The next Tetrad is 2032-2033.

> *The phenomena of 4 consecutive blood moons falling on Jewish holy days has occurred only 3 times since 1492 AD (which at that time, the 1493-1494 blood moons coincided with the Spanish Inquisition).*

The World's Stage

Today, in our political arena, we are witnessing war being waged in Europe and in the Middle East. Here in America, it's like watching an end-time movie on the wide-screen TV—but we are hurtling toward the fulfillment of end-time prophecies.

The Bible speaks of Israel in the end times; it is the focus of the world's attention. The end-time battle of Armageddon will be fought in Israel. Using spiritual eyes, we understand the true nature of this coming end-time battle: It reflects the battle being waged behind the scenes—in the spiritual realm. This end-time battle is judgment: God will erase the evil currently plaguing the planet.

The Rapture

Christ revealed the order of end-time events: The Rapture will occur years before Armageddon.[25] When Christ does appear in the sky, it will be an airlift operation for His kingdom off this Earth. Christ issued a prophecy of the Rapture during The Last Supper (as referenced in Chapter 18).

After Christ ascended into Heaven, He gave revelation to the apostle Paul, expounding upon His Rapture prophecy: At the time of the Rapture, all those in Christ's kingdom (who are dead in Christ and who are alive in Christ) will be transformed to receive eternal, spiritual bodies, suited for all eternity. It is our hope of glory: glorification with Christ. Paul prophesied:

> "[T]he Lord Himself will come down from heaven with a shout of command, with the voice of the archangel and with the [blast of the] trumpet of God, and the dead in Christ will rise first. Then we who are alive and remain [on the earth] will *simultaneously* be caught up (raptured) together with them [the resurrected ones] in the clouds to meet the Lord in the air, and so we will always be with the Lord!"[26]

It is only a matter of time before this come to pass. This day is the time of the Lord's intervention: the day of the Lord. It is when the sixth seal of the Book of Revelation opens. Glorification in Heaven follows.

And this is exactly what Christ revealed to John:

> "Then I [John] looked. And there was a great multitude which no one could count, from all nations and tribes and peoples and tongues, standing before the throne and before the Lamb, clothed with white robes, with palm branches in their hands. They cried out with a loud voice: 'Salvation belongs to our God

who sits on the throne, and to the Lamb!'"[27]

We are born anew of the Spirit of Christ— which transcends mortal death—and you along with it. If you have "Christ in you," then you have "the hope of glory": glorification with Christ.

This coming glorification is directly connected to another one of Christ's prophecies—which speaks to our generation:

"He who believes in Me, though he may die [is dead in Christ], yet shall he live. And whoever lives [is alive in Christ] and believes in Me shall never die."[28]

And now, this...

There will be some of us in this generation that will never taste death—because of the Rapture. In a moment of time, mortality will be transformed into immortality. Thus, Christ prophesied, "whoever lives and believes in Me shall never die."

"White Rabbit"

I end this Epilogue with Jefferson Airplane's "White Rabbit."

Here is the backstory: "Alice in Wonderland" went on her own spiritual journey. She did so by following her curiosity—which is represented by the "white rabbit." Grace Slick sang about this journey—which is awash with symbolism.

In an interview, Slick once said:

"I'm more interested in spirituality than religion. Religion involves a repetition of the same thing over and over again—which I don't do."[29]

"White Rabbit" is up to you to interpret.

White Rabbit

https://www.youtube.com/watch?v=rbVYQN0ziu0

Break on Through.

1. Romans 10:8–10.
2. John 8:12.

3. **John 11:27.**
4. **John 4:24.**
5. **1 John 4:16.**
6. **1 Peter 1:23.**
7. **2 Timothy 1:7.**
8. **Colossians 1:13.**
9. **Gal. 3:5.**
10. **Mark 16:17.**
11. **Mark 16:17.**
12. **1 Corinthians 12:8.**
13. **https://www.aarp.org/entertainment/television/info-2018/alice-cooper-newsinterview.html#:~:text=Alice%20Cooper%20says%20that%20before,persecuting%20the%20man%20he%20worships. Retrieval date: August 26, 2023.**
14. **Acts 2:17.**
15. **Isaiah 51:9.**
16. **Psalm 19:1–4.**
17. **https://nssdc.gsfc.nasa.gov/planetary/alignment.html._Retrieval date: June 24, 2022.**
18. **2 Peter 1:21.**
19. **Matthew 24:32–34.**
20. **Hosea 9:10.**
21. **Psalm 90:10.**
22. **Genesis 6:3.**
23. **See the article, "Generations in Prophecy: Israel" on my website.**
24. **Luke 21:25.**
25. **When Christ prophesied of His second coming to Israel (at the time of

Armageddon), He said, "Concerning that day and hour no one knows, not even the angels of heaven, but My Father only" (Matt. 24:36). This prophecy does not pertain to the Rapture (His return in the sky), but rather, His return to the Holy Land, Jerusalem (which is 7+ years after the Rapture: the time between Rev. 6:12 and 19:11). And, not knowing the "day and hour," is a reference to the Hebrew holy days. See my book, *The Mystery of God*. And see my website and the articles titled, "His Appearing," and "God's Blueprint: Holy Days."

26. 26. 1 Thessalonians 4:16, 17, *Amplified*.
27. Revelation 7:9, 10.
28. John 11:25, 26.
29. https://www.youtube.com/watch?v=OfooHF0Xao&t=695s. Retrieval date: February 12, 2024.

Don't Fear the Reaper

Psalm 40

A Psalm of King David

I waited patiently for the Lord; And He inclined to me, And heard my cry. He also brought me up out of a horrible pit, Out of the miry clay, And set my feet upon a rock, And established my steps.

He has put a new song in my mouth Praise to our God; Many will see it and fear, And will trust in the Lord.

Blessed is that man who makes the Lord his trust,

William Ayles, D.D.

And does not respect the proud, nor such as turn aside to lies. Many, O Lord my God, are Your wonderful works
Which You have done;
And Your thoughts toward us
Cannot be recounted to You in
order; If I would declare and
speak of them, They are more
than can be numbered.

Sacrifice and offering You did not
desire; My ears You have opened.
Burnt offering and sin offering You did not
require. Then I said, "Behold, I come;
In the scroll of the book it is written
of me. I delight to do Your will, O
my God, And Your law is within my
heart."

I have proclaimed the good news of righteousness
In the great assembly;
Indeed, I do not restrain my
lips, O Lord, You Yourself
know.
I have not hidden Your righteousness within my heart;
I have declared Your faithfulness and Your
salvation; I have not concealed Your
lovingkindness and Your truth From the great
assembly.

Do not withhold Your tender mercies from me, O Lord;
Let Your loving kindness and Your truth continually preserve me.

Don't Fear the Reaper

For innumerable evils have surrounded me;
My iniquities have overtaken me, so that I am not able to look up; They are more than the hairs of my head; Therefore my heart fails me.

Be pleased, O Lord, to deliver
me; O Lord, make haste to help
me!
Let them be ashamed and brought to mutual confusion
Who seek to destroy my life;
Let them be driven backward and brought to dishonor Who wish me evil.
Let them be confounded because of their shame, Who say to me, "Aha, aha!"

Let all those who seek You rejoice and be glad in You;
Let such as love Your salvation say continually,
"The Lord be magnified!"

But I am poor and needy;
Yet the Lord thinks upon me.
You are my help and my
deliverer; Do not delay, O my
God.

William Ayles, D.D.

THE END: PARADISE

In the Book of Revelation, Christ opened a portal of knowledge—enabling us to look into the future. He revealed to the apostle John the most intriguing scenes ever revealed regarding the coming creation: the new Heaven and new Earth. This new Earth is the home of Paradise:

> "Then I saw a new sky (heaven) and a new earth, for the former sky and the former earth had passed away (vanished), and there no longer existed any sea. And I saw the holy city, the new Jerusalem, descending out of heaven from God, all arrayed like a bride beautified *and* adorned for her husband; Then I heard a mighty voice from the throne *and* I perceived its distinct words, saying, See! The abode of God is with men, and He will live (encamp, tent) among them; and they shall be His people, and God shall personally be with them and be their God. God will wipe away every tear from their eyes; and death shall be no more, neither shall there be anguish (sorrow and mourning) nor grief nor pain any more, for the old conditions *and* the former order of things have passed away. And He Who is seated on the throne said, See! I make all things new.

> Also He said, Record this, for these sayings are faithful (accurate, incorruptible, and trustworthy) and true (genuine). And He [further] said to me, It is done! I am the Alpha and the Omega, the Beginning and the End. To the thirsty I [Myself] will give water without price from the fountain (springs) of the water of Life. He who is victorious shall inherit all these things, and I will be God to him and he shall be My son."[1]

This promise shall be fulfilled.
Thus, Christ implored us:

> "He who has an ear, let him hear what the Spirit says to the churches. To him who overcomes I [Christ] will give permission to eat of the tree of life, which is in the midst of the Paradise of God."[2]

God's Son has every interest in us… acquiring immortality and living for eternity in Paradise. He wants us to "overcome." What is it to "overcome" in this life? It is a matter of the heart. John said:

> "Everyone who believes that Jesus is the Christ is born of God, and everyone who loves the father [God] loves his child [Jesus] as well…. [E]veryone born of God overcomes the world. This is the

> victory that has overcome the world, even our faith. Who is it that overcomes the world? Only the one who believes that Jesus is the Son of God."[3]

Our Creator is interested in the heart: love... faith... belief. And our God wants us to know—with certainty—what our faith will bring forth in our future.

Our Lord and Savior compared our world to the coming world—and the insight He gave us about *infinity* is mind boggling:

> "The sons of this [world and present] age marry and [the women] are given in marriage; but those who are considered worthy to gain that [other world and that future] age and the resurrection from the dead, neither marry nor are given in marriage; and they cannot die again, because they are [immortal] like the angels (equal to, angel-like). And they are children of God, being participants in the resurrection."[4]

And finally, here are the staggering, closing visions of the new Earth:

> "I [John] saw no temple in the city, for the Lord God Almighty and the Lamb are its temple. The city has no need of sun or moon to shine in it, for the glory of God is its light, and its lamp is the

Lamb. And the nations of those who are saved shall walk in its light, and the kings of the earth shall bring their glory and honor into it. Its gates shall never be shut by day, for there shall be no night there. They shall bring into it the glory and the honor of the nations. No unclean thing shall ever enter it, nor shall anyone who commits abomination or falsehood, but only those whose names are written in the Lamb's Book of Life."[5]

"Then the angel showed me the river of the water of life, as clear as crystal, flowing from the throne of God and of the Lamb down the middle of the great street of the city. On each side of the river stood the tree of life, bearing twelve crops of fruit, yielding its fruit every month. And the leaves of the tree are for the healing of the nations. No longer will there be any curse. The throne of God and of the Lamb will be in the city, and his servants will serve him. They will see his face, and his name will be on their foreheads. There will be no more night. They will not need the light of a lamp or the light of the sun, for the Lord God will give them light. And they will reign for ever and ever."[6]

"I, Jesus, have sent My angel to you with this testimony for the churches. I am the

Root and the Offspring of David, the Bright and Morning Star."[7]

1. Revelation 21:1–7, *Amplified, Classic Edition.*
2. Revelation 2:7.
3. 1 John 5:1, 4, 5.
4. Luke 20:34–36, *Amplified.*
5. Revelation 21:22–27.
6. Revelation 22:1–5.
7. Revelation 22:16.

William Ayles, D.D.

THE PHOTOGRAPHS

Front Cover Photo
Hubble Space Telescope:
https://cdn.esahubble.org/archives/images/large/op 00609b.jpg.

Back Cover Photos
Hubble Space Telescope:
https://www.esa.int/ESA_Multimedia/Missions/Hubble_Space_Telescope/(offset)/100/(sortBy)/publishe d/(result_type)/images (page 3).

TimeLine International, Inc. logo photo
Hubble Space Telescope:
http://heritage.stsci.edu/2002/03/index.html (p. 21).

Interior Photos
Chapters 1 – 18: https://www.Alamy.com.

William Ayles, D.D.

Acknowledgments

I'd like to acknowledge God, who changed my life twice with (life-altering) divine intervention. I'd also like to acknowledge dear friends of mine who graciously accepted my request to review the manuscript: Emmy Wayne, Charles Floyd, and Gerry O'Hara. They all provided thoughtful insight—which enabled me to sense how the text speaks. Additionally, sections of this text are based on feedback I received from family and friends: Theresa Rivezzo spoke of Donna Summer and Justin Bieber; Michael Malvasi spoke of Bruce Springsteen; Dan Uitti spoke of "Sweet Sounds of Heaven," and my cousin Joey Ayles spoke of "The Sound of Silence," and how the band, Disturbed, covered it. Finally, Rita Reali, my editor, turned in yet another stellar performance, and Dan Uitti, my gifted webmaster, created the finished product, readying the book for production.

Don't Fear the Reaper

William Ayles, D.D.

Made in the USA
Middletown, DE
15 August 2024

59187265R00121